Welcome to the inside of this book. No, no, Mr. Noodle; not an *apology* for misanthropy, an <u>*anthology*</u> of misanthropy. It poses new muddles to riddle-me-rees which have been annoying mavens since *Noye's Fludde*. Some of these teasers have been conveniently placed on the page opposite for easy reference. You will find this grumpy volume a cutesy, knockabout rehash of words and notions that span times gone and times to be, conveniently sorted into three major divisions, viz, Conversations, Songs, and Sermons. All autoexplanatory. Ever striving toward coherence, *Misanthropology* pretends to be more than the sum of just what it is. Particularly garrulous and wont to cant, armed with neology, disjointed metaphor and malaprop, the book potshoots at the tin hats of straight talkers and ideologues, creating a refreshing symphony of rat-a-cackle. When you reach the finish line, you realize that things will ever be the same. Get started, and you're on your way. If your attention should wander off track, you will find the questions over there ☞ a helpful tool to redirect the apathetic bugger back to the plodding path of realization.

MIS
AN
THRO
POL
OGY

flo·ri·le·gi·um \ˌflōr-ə-ˈlē-jē-əm, ˌflȯr-, ˌflär-\ *n, pl* **flo·ri·le·gi**
\-jē-ə\ [NL, fr. L *florilegus* culling flowers, fr. *flori- + legere* t
gather — more at LEGEND] : a volume of writings : ANTHOLOGY

MISANTHROPOLOGY

A Florilegium of Bahumbuggery

Reneau H. Reneau

Illustrations by
Rius and Reneau-Santiago

donlázaro translations

Published by donlázaro translations

First printing, October 2003

Publisher's Cataloging-in-Publication
(Provided by Quality Books, Inc.)

Reneau, Reneau H.
    Misanthropology : a florilegium of bahumbuggery /
Reneau H. Reneau ; illustrations by Rius and
Reneau-Santiago.
    p. cm.
    LCCN 2003095160
    ISBN 0-9729549-0-2

    1. Philosophy--Miscellanea--Fiction. 2. Cosmology--
Miscellanea--Fiction. 3. Religion--Miscellanea--
Fiction. 4. Human evolution--Miscellanea--Fiction.
I. Rius. II. Reneau-Santiago. III. Title.

PS3618.E575M57 2003   813'.6
                        QBI03-700461

For Dali Xitlali

Past, Present, Future

Contents

Introduction

Misanthropology is an anthology of tripping forays into the essence of human being. Convinced that splash and garnish enhance palatability, Reneau gleefully tosses out a crunchy wordsalad, and then bakes up an alliterative collage and scrambles sentences to deliver an unexpected phrase, or a popup rhyme, even serving up some snappy one-liners for your fortune cookies (e.g. "a bigfat brainpan, the modest wimple of wisdom warms not"). But don't despair, it's not all one big happy pizza pie. There is a definitely cynical (if not exactly misanthropic) vein that laces this goulash, the ingredients of which actually span Reneau's lifetime. Recurring targets include hypocrisy and intolerance (Hooray. Hardly a courageous contrarian stance. Now *there's* a paradox). However, the embodiment of these targets, at least in the eyes of Reneau, seems to shift from one decade to the next. He is uncomfortable to find himself on a winning team, apparently of the opinion that once the fortress is taken, the oppressed and the oppressors simply switch roles. This, I suspect, explains his pessimism.

The *Songs* section is an updated and augmented revision of *Misanthropoesy,* published in Mexico in 1970. *Noel, Noel*, a statement on the babbittization of holy days, is not verse at all, but a pair of Christmas cards which Reneau designed and executed while at Ft. Lewis in 1955.

Alan Robinson, in his introduction to *Misanthropoesy,* commented: "Reneau H. Reneau is a parodist who achieves something more than parody. The ability to imitate other men's styles is no pastime for a mere literary parrot, and a successful parody is evidence of intelligence and subtlety; but brilliant imitation is one thing and poetry is another, for poetry rarely wears a borrowed shirt --- though poets frequently have to. The alert reader will spot the originals, among them Yeats, Eliot, Cummings, Blake, Millay; he will also hear, quite distinctly, the voice of Reneau, and it is at this point that parody becomes poetry. Not just other men's styles, but other men's words. As

Brubeck quotes Bach or Bartok, so Reneau borrows from a poem, a popular ballad, a nursery rhyme, and creates new resonances."

This assessment is most evident in the *Themes and Variations* segment of *Songs*. However, unexpected variations on "other men's words" do generously echo throughout the collection, indeed creating new resonance. When ideology is promoted here, it's not heavy-handed; Reneau calls his bouncy harangues "lyrical exposition." In standup cornball tradition, political utterance, from Richard III to Roosevelt and Lyndon Johnson, is zestfully impugned in these pages.

Moving on to *Conversations* and *Sermons,* his technique shifts to "declamatory conversation." In *Dummy Bilking*, Reneau sneers at scapegoatery. This rollicking essay starts out suspiciously like a revisionist assessment of drunken driving, but evolves into an elaborate dissection of deceit. It is here that cynicism reaches its cheerful apogee.

Where Are You? is yet another insight into the ethics of the news biz, with potshots at Philistine posturing. Flushing out more Philistines, in *Red is July* Reneau snipes at the education establishment. Other quarry lurks in the brush. If the *talentgang* conversation would appear to forgive the eccentricities and misdemeanors of productive genius, the *Stalin/Giuliani* essay appears to rein in license back to accountability.

Yellow Brick Road is straight polemic, aimed at what Reneau perceives to be an impercipient interpretation of some early Dakota editorials of L. Frank Baum (who wrote *The Wizard of Oz* later) that on the surface appear to have been a rallying cry for Indian holocaust. Reneau argues with convincing examples from his own past op-ed antics that Baum was simply acting as *provocateur,* employing "reverse psychology" before the term itself had been invented. References to the Wonderful Wiz pop up elsewhere in this volume. Here he is again in *Gentleman's Genie,* which otherwise is a leisurely and thoughtful conversation about what we want and what we *really* want, a quasi-theological inquiry into why so many prayers don't fly.

But *Excelsior* earns the accolade for Most Ambitious Entree on this platter of chatter. The initial launch appears to be space-opera parody, but events and badinage soon require more rumination and savoring for proper digestion, as Reneau attempts to introduce possible scenarios for the advent of the universe-as-we-know-it. The *Excelsior* conversation accounts for half of the "Notes" commentary. His original excuse for any notes at all was obviously to provide rules and regulations for the "Ergbolt the Blackbox" game he came up with to inaugurate the *Excelsior* expedition, but he seizes the open opportunity to provide "story behind the story" background, expose his inside jokes, and do a bit of posturing himself. Anyway, after some goofy banter *Excelsior* gets half serious and actually talks the cosmogony talk.

There will be moments when you may feel that Reneau's inspiration was *Finnegan's Wake*, but he assures me that it was in fact Shaw's *Don Juan in Hell* and Python's *Parrot Sketch*. I do not believe that Reneau is at all presumptuous in this comparison. *Misanthropology* is parsed in slapstick and highfalutin phrasing. This is a funny and a thoughtful experience, both nutritious in content and original in condiment.

When asked to write this introduction, I accepted with the stipulation that my name not be used to persuade reviewers to be courteous. Let the book fly on its own merit, said I, and when it makes it to the second printing, there'll be no question in your mind as to why. Then you can print my name if you like, but for now sign it

Simon Elron
Chair, Bionosis Studies
Okefenokee U.

CON
VER
SA
TIONS

Where Are You ?

For young Charlie Bugby, humdrumming along life's stagnant lagoons, fame and fortune had been nought but Wills -o'-the - Wisp. One crisp night, camping with his unfortunate family on Mt. Habitat, he fell into the clutches of opportune circumstance. The REST IS HISTORY. We are privileged to be able to reproduce here the original transcript of his fabled appearance on the *Where Are You?* show, when Charles Bugby's career *extraordinaire* in philanthropic journalism was baptized.

Where Are You?

The Players

Voice:
 urgently baritone
Harry Clootie:
 LEGENDARY talkshow host
Charles Bugby:
 je ne sais quoi guest

VOICE: Where are you? HERE you are! Here are WE with Harry Clootie! And here is HE -- Harree HARREEE!

CLOOTIE: Tonight we have something that DEFIES DESCRIPTION. You read about the ordeal of Charles Bugby and his family, only last week assaulted by a womaneating wildcat on Mount Habitat; how Bugby stayed ON THE SPOT to film the gluttonous, MADDENED cat as it attacked and devoured his defenseless wife and young daughter, leaving Bugby STRUGGLING FOR ANSWERS! Here tonight, with us, is Mr. Bugby and his descriptiondefying film, that YOU will experience for the FIRST TIME on the BIG TUBE. Let's hear it for this terribly IN CONTROL fellow, CHAZZZ BUGBEEE!

BUGBY: How *allez-vous* to all of you, from just me! My family would greet you, too, if they could, but as they look down from on *haut*, they know that you understand. I know they join me -- in *esprit* -- in hoping that you

will be jolted into action–– we'll tell you how later --- by what you are about to see, because if just one of *vous* out there can keep this from happening just one time, to just one *femme* in your family, then, as we cantillate at eastertide, "death has been swallowed up in *victoire*!" We will have all been indeed repaid a megafold, nay, a gigafold, *mesdames* and *messieurs* of the great TV --- as it were --- vidience! (chuckle).

CLOOTIE: A selfless, ELOQUENT utterance, Mr. Bugby. You're a regular French MAVEN! Perhaps you can summon the GUTSY BRAVADO it must take to SET US UP for the clip we're about to see. Tell us the DETAILS!! --- that's where the DEVIL resides, they say (chuckle). Get it OFF YOUR CHEST, so say the shrinks!

BUGBY: That is just what they speak, so to say, Mr. Clootie. Just talking about it makes me feels good all *œuvre*. It provides closure, you might *comment*, to bad experience. Well, let's get it on! We were camping in the Mt. Habitat Recreation Area, when one Tuesday morning -- I remember it was Tuesday because it was the second day of the week, "two's day," in Greco-Romano --- at 6am, just before dawn's crack, we were awakened by a savage roar outside the tent. My wife called out that a bear was messing about, so I crawled out of my sleeping bag, and like any derring-do daddy-o would doodly-do, investigated. As I stepped out of the tent, I spied a great puma, not a bear at all. My wife was wrong again. This *féroce* animal was snarling at me just a few feet from my very *nez*. I wiggled the flap of the tent to redirect his gaze (a tactic acquired from meticulous attention paid to the great toreadors of Spain) and leaped to the car, where I quickly opened the door and jumped in, in order to assess the situation from a vantage more secure.

The confused puma was still staring at the tent flap when my wife's *tête* poked thru, curiosity ever a woman's wont. Polly's tousled topsy then appeared, bless her gobbled-up little *cœur*.

CLOOTIE: Little did they dream that they were about to take their FINAL BOW with 15 MINUTES OF FAME in one shocking video! But tell us, Mr. Bugby, how would you DESCRIBE YOUR EMOTIONS at this point? American inquirers have a RIGHT TO KNOW!

BUGBY: My emotions were a roiling *omelette*, oh my *frère*. Of course, I was worried sick about my wife and child --- can you blame me? But at the same time, deep down, I was honestly grateful to Mr. Man Upstairs that it was them and not *moi*. You know what they say, if it's between *moi* or my *grand-mère*, ta-ta, grandma!

CLOOTIE: Such candor is a RARE COMMODITY! Such sublime FREUDIAN INSIGHT! Well, like they like to say, when the GRIM REAPER knocks, he *knocks down the door!* Any FINAL QUOTEABLES from your wife?

BUGBY: She had no time for histrionics, *Monsieur* Clootie. Polly did say, "Help me, Daddy!" or something equally *pathétique*. I couldn't hear very *bien* with the windows rolled up. Polly was my little *fille*.

CLOOTIE: Words so like a DAGGER TO YOUR HEART! Surely, little Polly Bugby WILL BE SORELY MISSED. She was so SPECIAL.

BUGBY: You *touche* me to the *vite,* Mr. Clootie. You are really *bon* at soundbiting those things that poor blokes like *moi* only feel. But I know that right now they are safe and *sonore* from all alarm, at the Happy Hunting Ground up there in the air, as they say *en province*. Well, the *vorace* animal jumped at them and started to eat them up! I shouted for them to come to the car, but I guess they couldn't hear me, with the windows shut.

CLOOTIE: Didn't it occur to you to THROW CAUTION TO THE WINDS and attack the wildcat?

BUGBY: *Vous*'re kidding! I only play on a flat *champ*. Of course, I thought about it. I used to watch Tarzan on television. But, hey, his *mère* was a monkey (chuckle)! Get *véritable*! "Between thought and action there is an abyss," said a wise French guy. "That abyss is *prudence,*" sez I.

CLOOTIE: A noble urge, realized or not, Bugby! Hey, if you had yielded to urge, you'd be in YESTERDAY'S OBITS and not on TODAY'S NATIONAL TV! But we must MOVE ON. How did it occur to you to film the proceedings?

BUGBY: Cold *logique*, Mr. Clootie, convinced *moi*. After all, what else could I do? A great revelation came to me that I was an instrument in the hands of *Dieu* --- that's the French "God," in case *vous* didn't know. By recording this unfortunate incident in my life, others might learn how to avoid such mishaps in their own *misérable* lives. Stay tuned; as a public service, we'll show you the way. But I do digress. In the car, I noticed the camcorder on the seat beside *moi*. My lifelong ambition to report heart-wrenching, relevant news was in my clutch! I swallowed hard, and, for the greater *bon*, made myself forget that it was my own *famille* that I would be shooting.

CLOOTIE: Yes, the SHOW MUST GO ON! Now we shall see, for the first time anywhere, the Bugby tape! For real redmeat violence, it's a SOCK IN THE JAW! And it's a WHERE ARE YOU? exclusive! The authentic, unabridged, ON THE SPOT footage you are about to see is a MONUMENT TO REALISM in journalism. Lights, camera, VIOLENCE!

(The videotape is shown. Gasps and groans from the audience are audible.)

CLOOTIE: (Gulp!) Great BALLS OF FIRE, Mr. Bugby. Your tape is not for the queasy in any WAY SHAPE OR FORM! Your zoom-ins were quite effective, by the way.

BUGBY   I strive for excellence, Mr. Clootie! Or, *excellence,* as we French-o-phones would have it. Did you notice the big teeth? Like Red Riding Hood's *grand-mère*, eh?

CLOOTIE: BOY, HOWDY! But on a SERIOUS NOTE, Mr. Bugby, I understand there was the usual police investigation. I know this is a TOUCHY-FEELY topic to bring up, but of course you were cleared of any impropriety, like criminal negligence; am I right, OR AM I RIGHT?

BUGBY: *Au contraire*, oh *mon* bro (chuckle)! I was awarded the Smileyface for Quickthink. My videotape was all the investigation needed, and saved the cops *beaucoup* time and cash. Our men in *bleu* are really into professional razzadoodle; naturally, when you're not taping *them*, they're such limelight dodgers. But they know how important it is to remain *objectif* when confronted with personal tragedy, no matter how *personnel*, no matter how *tragique*. And news reporters must likewise be sentinels of *pierre.* While I was shooting, I felt myself a part of the camcorder, *histoire's miroir*!

CLOOTIE: A TECHNICAL QUESTION, Mr. Bugby. At 6am, at this time of year, the sun's not up yet, and there's not enough natural light to produce such CRYSTAL-CLEAR images! How did you get around that seemingly UNSURMOUNTABLE OBSTACLE?

BUGBY: Glad you asked, Mr. Clootie. I used the bright headlights. It took just a jiffy to switch them on; Mr. *gourmet* Puma was too busy to notice. I want the civilized world to know I have offered a big reward for his capture, *mort* or alive! He will pay for his terrible crime against *humanité*, eternally recorded on videotape, for all to vicariously feel the *horreur*!

CLOOTIE: And what will be your NEXT MOVE, Mr. Bugby? Now that you are a celebrity, will you seek new career as a MEDIA MUCKRAKER?

BUGBY: Definitely my humdrum *vie* as a computer programmer is *finie*, Mr. Clootie. I have always felt that my destiny would be more transcendental than one bogged down in bits and bytes. I want to join the ranks of those who sacrifice *tout* to open humanity's *yeux* so they can see what is really going on around them! Around the corner! In the shadows! In the *Blanche Maison*! *Vous* know, some anonymous gentleman phoned me with the tip that he was going to kill the President at the Redskins game. I went, zoom-lens ready, to shoot the shocking event, grimly prepared to make Zapruder look like an *amateur*! But the Prez didn't even show. It was just another crank call, *je* think. But that goes with the *territoire.*

CLOOTIE: Did you notify the police? They would WANT TO KNOW!

BUGBY: But *non*, Mr. Clootie. We don't make history, we only record it. And you should know very well that we never divulge our sources. They might dry up on *nous*. We're like priests; finking is not in our job description. And opportunity's *fenêtre* doesn't stay open very long. I wanted to go to Kosovo to film *atrocités*, but you saw what happened there. Suddenly there was no *guerre*. Thank *Dieu*, of course.

CLOOTIE: Monsieur Bugby, only a few BREATHTAKING MOMENTS remain! I understand you have a CAN'T-BE MISSED announcement for all well-intentioned citizens interested in making our mountains a LEVEL PLAYING FIELD, and in combatting PUMA TERRORIST ATTACKS on our women!

BUGBY: *Oui oui*, we are ready to help *vous*! I have formed an advocacy group, Americans Against Ravenous Girleating Hellcats, or AARGH, for short, and *oui oui oui!* we are accepting donations at this time.

CLOOTIE: I know that all our RED-BLOODED teletomatoes (chuckle) will want to participate, Mr. Bugby. Tell me, can JUST ANYBODY send in a generous donation?

BUGBY: No dollar will be turned away, Mr. Clootie. Of course, the more there are, the *plus jolis* are we! But naturally we can accomplish so much, much more with higher denominations, that is to say, bigger bucks! And to show our gratitude, for every $100 pledge I'll send a you lock of Polly's golden *cheveu*. And for a $1,000 pledge, you'll get one of my wife's teeth! Mr. Finicky Puma didn't gobble up everything. These collector's gems will command thousands on eBay before you can blink a *oeil*! And for every dollar you send me, Harry Clootie gets half for his own worthy causes, many of which involve needy ladies. So it's a win-win-win *occasion*! Loosen up those moneybelts and get the C-notes to *nous* so we can wipe out this scourge! The wife you save could be your own (chuckle)! Volunteers at AARGH headquarters are waiting at this moment for your pledge. Remember, no shipping and handling charge applies. And there is no tax! Don't let down the *femmes*!

CLOOTIE: Yes, teleladies and telegents, SEIZE THE DAY and make your cash talk. Not only is there *no tax*, your donations are not TAX DEDUCTIBLE! You'll be fighting SHOULDER-TO-SHOULDER with Uncle Sam against national debt and TERRORISM! Join Charlie Bugby in his NOBLE CRUSADE, let your money mouth your outrage at these wild animals roaming our mountains, and sign up today with AARGH! Call the number flashing on your screen RIGHT THIS MINUTE! Every minute you lose is a MINUTE LOST! Here are WE, awaiting your call!

VOICE: WHERE ARE YOU?

A Gentleman's Genie

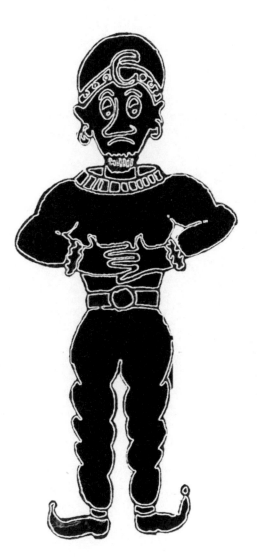

In the name of Allah the Most Merciful, onceupona time in Genielandia, John Genie awoke, yawned, and looked at the perpetual calendar on his wall to see that thousands of years had passed since he was last summoned to duty. "Who can it be this time," he said to himself, "and what foolish wishes will he invoke to hasten his misery and untimely demise? Can anything be done to hone his wisdom so he may benefit from this most precious gift which is about to be thrust upon him?" The answer will be found in the pages which follow. May Allah, who alone understands the desires deep within our hearts, be praised.

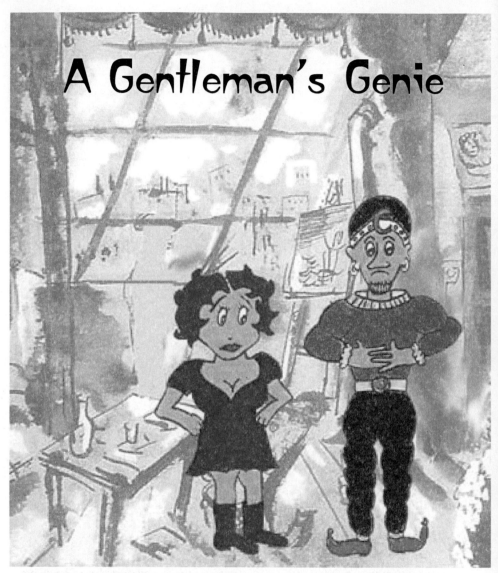

A Gentleman's Genie

SPEAKING ROLES: Simon Elron *programmer with literary pretensions;* John Genie *miracle man;* Yam Snosnibor *advisor to Simon;* Simone Elron *clever wife of Simon;* Sgt. Flezzie *singing bobby, cameo role oft played with mucho gusto by Luis Buñuel;* Chorus of Omnuiscients

PRELIMINARY: Macdonald's Used Bookstore on Mission Street

CHORUS: Simon Elron has always been attracted to secondhand bookstores. There is something about them that you just don't see in the outside world. Every volume a vista, a pouring out of ideas studied or imagined; developed, expounded, and signed by someone who thought he had something to say: for money, for fame, for recognition, for influence, for sharing, for exculpation, foir inspiration, for amusement! And if you fontfreeze what you have to say, the temptation is to be more fastidious about it. You know you are writing for the eyes of tomorrow as well as for the eyes of now, and that's a heap o' scrutinizin'.

Simon says that if someone plunked down the cash years ago to actually publish these words, the odds are that there is interest of compounded value in these no longer stylish tomes. As Simon likes to remark to those who respect his opinion, since the invention of the written word, mental man hasn't shown any improvement at all; as a matter of fact, he avers with a wink, the yester the bester. He then convincingly draws unkind comparisons between latter-day presidents and the philosopher kings. Today Simon is browsing away a chilly afternoon. Actually, he has come to look for information on ancient Holy Land manuscripts which might help him decipher a mysterious scroll he had purchased the week before at the Goodwill. He and a figure at the cash-box, wrapped in a greatcoat with only an icy nose projecting through the upturned collar, presumably old Macdonald himself, are the only ones seen in the store. For years Macdonald has been Simon's encyclopedia, oracle, and father-confessor; old Mac's advice is sought on every subject. Last week it was about parlor tricks; but yesterday, Simon had asked him to translate the title of his newly acquired scroll, carefully copied to a Post-It note. Mac had pleaded that while the words were weirdly familiar, they were quite undecipherable, implying an error in the transcription. Annoyed, Simon comes today to research on his own. The store is large, with a high ceiling that permits a mezzanine in the rear, but principally serves to allow all the warm air to rise and pull in cold air from the street. Mr. Mac is never caught without a greatcoat. Simon is in the "Occult" section in the rear of this dimly-lit emporium, and he bumps into a book enticingly projecting from the shelf, with a title that buzzes for his attention: "Prestidigitation for Clumsies." The scroll is completely forgotten. As is his wont while in a bookstore, Simon is talking to himself, and exclaims, with childlike candor:

SIMON: Just the volume for me! How jolly fortuitous to find just what I require to be the life of the office party! Aha! A card trick that finds a selected card behind a bystander's unsuspecting ear! Amazing! A bunch of colored handkerchiefs coming out of his nose? IMPOSSIBLE! But what is this tucked away between chapters? A bit of dry parchment with hand-lettered runes? What can it mean? How fortunate that I took that elective course in Runology. Let me see: *To make a wish-granting genie appear, just say, with childlike candor: Kadabra, Sesameanie, I conjure me a genie. ...* WOWIE! A cloud of smoke! A cyranosed, turbaned gent looms in the gloom! Hello, you look like a genuine genie!

JOHN: I am John Genie, o fortunate mortal. Thou hast managed to say the conjuring phrase with proper attitude, which no one has done for ten thousand years. Lucky thou; if thou hadst muffed the chance, thou wouldst have disappeared in a puff and a whiff. But no matter. I am at thy beck. Tell me what thou dost want of me. Nothing that thou canst imagine will be denied thee.

SIMON: Whew. I'm in a state of shock, or maybe denial already! Are you really there? And even if you say, "Yea, verily," what proof is that?

JOHN: Good thinking, Simon. But what doth it matter if I'm really here? Thou thinkst I am. Enjoy the moment. Who knoweth what bringeth the morn? *Carpe* the bloody *diem*!

SIMON: Hold on, o *image fantastique*. Hyperbole in your pronouncement: ten thousand years? Aladdin, a prior client, if I'm not mistaken, is not two thousand years old! Anachronism in your costume: the Robinson's-May pricetag is showing on your turban! *Discolpati.*

JOHN: Foolish Simon, why must I justify what thou see'st with thine eyes and hear'st with thine ears? Aladdin is just an old wife's tale. And I just got the turban because I wouldn't look like a genie to thee without it. Thou see'st a genie before thee in accordance with thine expectations. Wish away. That's why I'm here.

SIMON: Not so fast, John Genie. I am conversant with the literature of genies. I have concluded that discretion and deliberation, rather than impulse and haste, have better chance for optimum advantage. How many wishes am I granted? The traditional three?

JOHN: The limit is infinite! Wish away. Test me.

SIMON: Very well. *Let's see you pull many colored*

handkerchiefs from my nose! ... WHAT TH'! I can't believe my orbs! You DID it! OK, John Genie, let's get down to serious business. Tell me what our relationship should be. How do I summon you? Must I repeat the rune stuff?

JOHN: Not unless thou so desireth. I wouldn't recommend it. Thou mightst not strike proper attitude every time. Thou mayst determine a more facile procedure.

SIMON: OK, JG. *Obey any of my subsequent commands preceded by "Simon says..." Ignore any command without this preface.*

JOHN: It shall be thus, oh my master, but allow me to proffer thee gratuitous opinion this one time. Thou must hack it without mine advice from now on. Thou shouldst tell me when a command ends. If thou sayeth "Simon says, I want a BLT, dammit!" I don't think thou wantest an execrated sandwich. Thou hast to think of these things if thou'rt to be a successful wisher. And thou definitely needest an assistant to help thee decide what thou really wantest. Although the franchise granted thee does not permit my assuming this role, I can provide thee with a competent opiner if thou but sayeth the word.

SIMON: Splendid counsel, o genie o' mine. *Simon says, wishing sequence will end with "over and out." Over and out.* You know, I can't thank you enough for the free advice. These sessions do need to be planned. I must have an advisor at my elbow. *Simon says, give me a full-time, wise and honest consultant, over and out.* And you don't need to hang around after granting my wishes. I'm sure you've got genie things to do.

CHORUS: From this moment on, John appears on the "Simon says" cue and disappears on "over and out," usually without comment, presumably to get to work and get out of the way. This time, the job is accomplished in short order, and a smartly attired and manicured matron, coordinated from wig to boots, in an outfit that would scream *aplomb!* and *seemliness!* to any discerning onlooker, appears from a side aisle. Simon is impressed.

YAM: Shazam! Here I am, Yam Snosnibor. Yam I am. *Kaif halak*? How may I advise you today?

SIMON: Wow! *Al ham dulillah*. At my beck a can-do counselor. Yam, advice is required on how to maximize advantage of my astonishing ability to have all my wishes granted. I don't want to mess up. You see, I'm a real booklooker, and have spectated many sagas of simps who are granted these powers and, as I recall, most of them end up badly. I intend to go about my wishing as a serious job, requiring careful thought and judicious planning, ever consistent with self-interest. Do you read my dictum?

YAM: Roger, blueDodger! I suggest you create a council of two to advise you: your wife and myself. Anything you do affects your wife, and her reaction will itself affect you, possibly altering the effect of the wish itself. You listen to us and make your decision. You can reject our suggestions if you want to, but of course I wouldn't advise that. Why don't you wish your wife here now?

SIMON: Yes, yes! Now do we pirouette on the big toe. *Simon says, let here Simone appear! Over and out.*

JOHN: Thou hast spoken, master. *Voilà.*

YAM: *Allah akbar*! Here's your wife.

SIMONE: Aha! Here you are, you bookworm. I knew I'd find you wasting your time at Macdonald's. Who's the hussy?

SIMON: Simone! Wife, companion, miraculously you do appear before me! Let me explain to you a thing or two. You're on my advisory council! This is Yam, and you and she will advise me on how to best express my wishes. You see, a genie has offered to grant me any wish I come up with. This is a gold-filled opportunity for us, kid! Just watch this! *Simon says, pull many colored handkerchiefs from my wife's nose! Over and out.*

SIMONE: .... INCREDIBLE! This is really an impossible dream. Now, what about asking for money? That should be a snap for your genie pal, and I could really advise you as to how to spend it wisely.

YAM: You know, I'd be a derelict advisor if I didn't tell you we'd better mosey on out of here. We can chit-chat on the way. We're in a book store, you know; folks wander in, nosey old Mac will wake up and overhear something. Out we go, one-two, one-two, off to your pad. Lead the way. But we really need a conference room for deliberations. It's easy enough to wish for one, and then wish that we were there. Let's talk about it. Sound off, one, two...

CHORUS: As they march down Mission Street, past
warehouses, bars, and flophouses, they turn
left on 7th street, left into an alley-with-a-
name, into a curtained glass-paned door, up
some stairs, and into a vaulted-ceiling, genie-
ready loft, wallpapered with shelves of books
from Macdonald's. This is home to Simon and
Simone.

MAIN EVENT: The Artsy Flat of Simon and Simone Elron

SIMONE: We should decide first what amenities this conference
room should offer. Furnishings? Location? There are so
many details. Genies are like computers, they have to
be programmed step by step. Well, here we are home.
Squad halt. After you, Mme. Yam.

YAM: Not so! No need to micromanage the genie. He's got to
be good at filling in blanks. You didn't supply any
details about me, did you? Are you satisfied with the
merchandise or not? Say, nice digs you've got here.

SIMONE: Thanks. Our house is your temporary parking space.
Have a lent chair. Shouldn't Simon be more specific in
his wishes?

YAM: Specific to the extent that he avoids ambiguity. But
consider: a competent gentleman's gent understands
pretty well what his master wants when he makes an
abbreviated request. Can a gentleman's genie do no
less? I suggest that you command John to grant your
wishes within the context of your life experience, but if
there is any doubt as to intent, to so inform you before

granting, so you can convene council to determine how to express correctly your desire.

SIMON: On your twirly-toe, as usual, sensible Yam. *Simon says, let us be in a comfortable place we can use as a conference room. All my wishes are to be parsed in accordance with my tastes. And if there's any doubt as to my intent let me know so I can clarify. Over and out....* What's this? We haven't budged! What's the problem? We're still in my living room!

SIMONE: You see? We're falling into the pattern. *La maledizione!* We do have to micromanage this tunnelvision genie.

YAM: Hold on! The genie has hammered the nail on its blunt! What more comfortable spot than your own living room? And you know right where the thunderbox is.

SIMON: Who would of thought of that other than a sensitive and concerned genie? Another wham-bam, Yam! Now for serious deliberation. How about wishing for a pile of money for starters? Then we can TAKE IT AND SPEND IT! What says comrade Yam?

YAM: Well, let's think about it. We can't just wish for cash Where would it come from? John'd either have to steal it or counterfeit it. And remember that bills have serial numbers.

SIMONE: Gold is easily transformed into cash. No serial number on a nugget. And it's in the ground, waiting to be found.

YAM: Somebody or something has title to most acres and plots and lots, and the earth beneath. For John to come up with a retroactive easement would inevitably involve an illegal act.

SIMONE: Surely John could figure a way around that. But why not get gold from under the ocean? Who owns that?

SIMON: Or just have John create it out of something else. Just realign the atomic structure of something nobody wants, like garbage. Imagine that! Au out of P-U, har har.

YAM: We still have the problem of converting it into currency. They'll be wondering where you got it. They'll report it to the authorities.

SIMONE: Oh, shut up. Let John figure out the details. He can keep it licit. Why are you obliged to invent complications? On to *Go*, and a pot of legal tender! But you know? Come up with a better alternative to your *"in accordance with my tastes"* bit.

SIMON: Good thinking, Simone, rib-o'-me-own. How about *"Don't allow any of my wishes to cause us any collateral grief. And bring me a suitcase of big bills."*

SIMONE: Sounds doable to me, dear. We can use those big bills to pay outstanding bills while we dream up other wishes. Any objection now, Yam?

YAM: Sounds great, but smells bad. We'll have to articulate some wishes for appropriate security, and determine access to the cash. You can't just plunk a million bucks into your bank account, now can you? With this brand of *ad hoc* planning you'll be summoning John just to get us out of each jam the previous wish got us into.

SIMON: Good grief, doesn't my collateral damage clause take care of that?

YAM: I suspect that it will only take care of problems involving the fabrication of the suitcase with the cash, not with problems you may provoke with subsequent transfer of the cash. Look, don't wish for a suitcase of big bills. Wish for a big bank account, with no collateral damage. Better yet, wish independently that the "collateral damage" clause apply to all your wishes.

SIMON: Done! *Simon says, may none of my wishes provoke any collateral grief for me or mine. I want a big buck bank account. Over and out.*

JOHN: Very good indeed, master. Take this lottery ticket. I'll see that it wins tonight and thou canst redeem it tomorrow. Just give them thy ticket and account number. Now, I've got a neat trick I'd like to show thee.

SIMON: A winning lottery ticket! Stand and ovate, ladies, a genie genius! A great solution to our dilemma. Thanks anyway John, but let's not warp your wand from overuse. You can forget the trick for now. Get lost in Genieland. I'll call you when I need you.

YAM: It seems I insist on being a perennial party-pooper, but why do you need money at all? What can money buy you that you can't just wish for? With plastic, you don't need cash, and John Genie beats a credit card. Forget the lottery ticket. Or better, give it to the March of Dimes.

SIMON: Yam, you're really in a hard loop, ma'am. Are we deliberating too much, or what? We seem to be talking to death this really useful talent that has been conferred upon me. And yet... I dunno. What you say makes sense. Why should I waste time manipulating money to achieve objectives that I can accomplish without it?

SIMONE: Maybe, just maybe, the manipulation of money is itself part of the fun.

YAM: On the other hand, just maybe not. But whatever. Go ahead and turn in the lottery ticket and have fun writing checks and paying taxes. Of course, you could wish for an honest accountant and let him take care of all that, but it seems to me that you're wasting wishes in order to create complications.

SIMONE: How do we pay the rent? The gas bill? The groceries? And on and on? Wish that everybody just give us anything we want for nothing? Wouldn't this attract gossipy attention? Or is that taken care of by the collateral damage clause?

YAM: Let me suggest a scenario. We transport your living quarters, or a reasonable fax thereof, with us and all, to another dimension or whatever, appropriately cocooned from danger, with amenities miraculously supplied by John. Any time we need to physically go anywhere, we just wish we were there. No need to mess with intermediaries or their currency at all.

SIMON: What would we see out of the window in this dimension? Would we hear the birds on the telephone poles? The clang of the trolleys? A sense of life going on as usual? Silly me. A piece of putty for John, I reckon. I'll just have to specify it that way. Sounds like a safe, comfy way to set up for business. *Simon says, let this flat and its contents be situated in a place not accessible to living things other than present company. May all life's necessities, and goods and services currently available, be supplied, as required, by John Genie. And may it appear that nothing has changed. Over and out.*

CHORUS: John silently appears and disappears on cue. Nothing appears to have changed.

YAM: What a genie! What mental peace. Here we are, strategically defended, and where we can comfortably deliberate. And everything looks the same! I suggest that before we get down to serious deliberation, anyone who has to use the bathroom, does so at this time. As for yours truly, a quick trip is not amiss. I'll return shortly. This way, I presume? This will give you an opportunity to discuss my performance behind my back. I have every confidence that my job skills have exceeded your wildest standards.

SIMON: Why, yes it's over there; miss it you can't, miss. The light's a click-on, over the toilet. We'll get John to fix that to make it more accessible.

SIMONE: I'm starting a list. That'll be on it. Pssst, Simon, while I do think Yam overall is an asset, I suggest that *chadari* attire would be more appropriate for one of her persuasion, not her *Tia Pelucas* apparatus. You might suggest it to her. John can provide her *chadari* in a fingersnap.

SIMON: Shame, shame, politically *gauche* Simone. Yam looks like a snappy Century 21 consultant. She's not a medieval vizier, advising on camel acquisition. JG fitted her in accordance with my expectations, as is his wont. But she is taking a long time in there.

SIMONE: I've got a great idea for a particularly useful wish. How about John fixing it up so we don't have to go to the bathroom at all? It's messy and smelly, and think of all the time we'd save, engaged in mind improvement instead of just peeing and pooing. If we had used the time we spend on the thundermug reading the *Great Books of the Western World*, we'd have finished *Forever Amber* by now. Oh oh, chiggers, Simon, here comes Yam.

YAM: My wax-free soundscoops picked up your tootles, toots. What can you be thinking? How would that work? Your bodies would completely consume and utilize all victuals? Your digestive tract would, to put it tastefully, have to undergo such a radical update that you'd have something like ... bionic guts! Could you handle it? And yet there's another angle. Let's put all shame aside and gobbletalk. I just walked out of your thunderbox. When I went in I felt anxious, with what might be described as a pressing need to jettison toxic elements. How do you think I feel now?

SIMON: Relieved?

SIMONE: At peace with the world?

YAM: Yes, yes! *Allah akhbar*! A tranquil blessing of being. A moment of aloneness, the madding kerfuffle locked outside, a time to purge one's face of masks, to reflect and relax. And you want to do away with this boon-o'-boons? I don't think so.

SIMONE: I may have been a bit hasty, Yam. Just an idle thought. Can you ever forgive me? I'll come up with a workable concept yet, you can bet on it.

SIMON: Why, I myself have oft observed that a spirited BM is one of life's minor victories on a horizon of major defeats. But enough of this mucky palaver. Our horizon will soon bloat with victories! Let's get it on! How about wishing for an idea for a good wish?

YAM: Please, Simon. Have you so little confidence in my professional competence? Why do you think John has lent me to you? It would be just too embarrassing for me to have to recur to John for his opinion. Opinions are in my job description, not his. Remember how he kvetched at having to give you free advice? May I remind you, you haven't asked me to suggest a good wish yet. You just ask me to comment on your bad ideas. But now that you're interested in positive input, how about knowledge?

SIMON: Yes, now we can know everything we have a right to know! I've always wanted to know if Oswald was really just a cog in an interesting conspiracy to kill Kennedy.

SIMONE: Yes, and I'm dying to know colorful details about Princess Diana's sex life!

YAM: You're kidding.

SIMON: No, we're not. You're not going to party-poop us this time, Yam. *Simon says, give us all details relevant to the assassination of President Kennedy and the sex life of Princess Diana, over and out.*

JOHN: This tape hath everything relevant to the assassination of President Kennedy, from its genesis in Oswald's head to its execution by Oswald's hand. I'm glad thou didst not ask for information as to the investigation of the assassination; that would have been voluminous. This other tape contains visuals of all sexual activity of Princess Diana. Thou'rt hereby advised of possible legal problems by virtue of thy possession of this material. However, any collateral damage can be deflected by subsequent successful legal defense, as required. But is it really worth it? What dost thou learn with this information, anyway? Yam, thou'rt doing a sloppy job. And Simon, my trick is of more ennobling calibre than the sensational crap Yam is pushing.

YAM: Pish, John Genie. I'm not in the chain of command. I'm only staff, remember? Simone, you see what you get me into? Are you really going to take the time to look at all that Diana sex stuff? What do you expect to see of any novelty? If this is your notion of knowledge, may Allah be merciful.

JOHN: Honest-to Allah, Simon, magic is also *divertissement intellectuel*! And my trick is a doozie. Humor me.

SIMON: John, I said forget your silly flimflam. *Sayonara, mon ami.* As soon as I've got the time, I'll watch this Kennedy tape from *Go* to *Boardwalk.* As for you, silly Simone, I would like all to note that my tape is a really serious document that will settle the conspiracy theory once and for eternity. Historians will love me when I come out with my book, *Who Really, Really,* Really *Killed JFK?*

YAM: Wrong again. Historians will hate you. You will have terminated a major industry. No more grants, no more research, investigations, expense accounts, book advances, lecture circuits, debates, magazine articles exploiting a *nuance nouveau*, movies, tapes, reruns... you've killed it all. And what do you have in return? A smug notoriety?

SIMON: You think you're so smart, Yam. How do you know what I'll write? Yes, I'll know the truth, because I suppose that John has supplied me with all the relevant facts, but no one else will know that. How can you prove that Oswald was not in a plot by taking pictures of him not plotting? On the other hand, knowing all the relevant facts will enable me to weave a startling *j'accuse* tale of circumstantial conjecture, fingering some evangelical icon -- how about the Pope? -- forged to these facts with convincing innuendo. I will appease the people's righteous hunger for the unhumdrum! I shall make a bombblast contribution to publishing. The artist's milieu is suggestion and insinuation, not hairy reality. Imagine if the Great Masters were just passport photogs! Fie! When I go to my high school reunion, my old peers will oooh! They will ooompaaah! And about that knowledge angle. Why not have John just download to my brain the *Great Books of the Western World*? And anything else that would lend me erudition?

YAM: Simon, Simon. As fast as you can, repeat after me: "O-wah-tay-goo Siam."

SIMONE: Deceitful Yam! You seek to entrap and embarrass my husband in front of his wife! What has he done to merit such scorn?

SIMON: Simone, dearest rib, I get the point of her thrust. She is reminding me that an idiot savant is more idiot than savant. Any pig can swig; only a connoisseur can taste. It's just a question of my framing the wish correctly. Say, how could John possibly have filmed all this stuff, anyway?

YAM: Nothing that happens is lost in the cosmos. All is recorded, in the rocks, so to speak, and when unscrambled, can be replayed like a phonograph record. So be careful what you do, if you don't want your grandkids snickering at your indiscretions. But just hold it right there! Before you summon John and make a fool of me again! You are right about the consequence of merely downloading books to your head. But even framing the question in the most advantageous light might not be advantage enough, if you consider ramifications. In order for you to understand the Great Books, you would have to be able to relate to another universe of knowledge and ideas, that would in effect require that you, the Simon you know and love as-is, become a stranger to Simon the erudite.

SIMONE: O shrew untamed! My Simon is a veteran ogler of literature! All his life, he looks at books! He even wrote an essay for Subject A called *Shakespeare Was a Really, Really,* Really *Profound Writer.*

YAM: Do exit the pulpit, Simone. Your Simon traveled from *The Cowardly Lion of Oz* to *Kiss the Blood Off My Hands*, with similar literary junkets in between. His mind is unequipped for the big boggle, bless his little college pedigree. A man's mind is defined by the books he actually reads on his own, not by the ones he's assigned to read, nor --- need I say it --- the ones he thinks he should read, or displays on his shelf. Why, just to prepare Simon for *Tom Jones* would require major brain surgery.

SIMONE: Such sublime candor! Methinks you have just sublimely candored yourself out of a posh post, Yamadam. Or can you tell me if J. Jacques Rousseau was any more successful at promoting family values than R. Plumly Thompson? The answer, *mein schmo,* is no. *Nyet, nyet,* Nanette! Send Yam flying to Uzbekistan, Simon. *Udge, Budge, go to Mudge! Udger, Budger, she's a Mudger!*

SIMON: Simone, my darling Philistine! John Genie could not conjure me a more loyal mate. But consider: my ego needs unvarnished advice, even as my id feeds on your varnished support. The two of you I need, I do! Brain surgery? Maybe it's just a tufflove way of saying "exorcise the engrams in the attic." Well, Simon the child would not know or understand Simon the man. And growing up was not that painful. I still remember some of the experiences of Simon *enfant.* So a *Great*

Books Simon would just be an improved version. Don't you think?

YAM: But there is a cushion of time from child to man. Understanding all the *Great Books* would change your perception. It would affect your subsequent wishes --- if any. I am reminded, my friend, of a story you read in high school, about a weary Russian who digested so many books that he concluded that life was indeed stale and flat, and he came to an unprofitable end. And yet I did recommend knowledge. But perhaps I should have phrased it differently. You might wish for a desire to seek knowledge, which would require only a slight tinkering with your psyche. And the time required for you to absorb this knowledge would allow time for you and Simone to adjust to the new and improved Simon.

SIMONE: What? Extend this talkalot to an interminable thinkathon? What are we waiting for? Why aren't you advising Simon as to specific wishes, and why is he not wishing away, feeling wise, gratified, happy, feared, worshipped, etc, as a consequence of these on-the-mark wishes?

SIMON: Of course! The top-down approach! That's the wishlist! The id got it did, kid. My wishes should be so redacted within obviously worthy general objectives as to obtain for us all of the above and more (write it down, Simone): ... 1) smarts, 2) luxury, 3) love, 4) fun, 5) gratification, 6) fame, 7) vengeance, 8) obeisance, 9) eternal life, 10) glorification! Did we leave anything out?

YAM: Here we go again. First of all, your list has holes in it.

You can be smart but not prudent. You can live in luxury and be bored of it. I could go on. Eternal life! You could be an eternally fresh vegetable. Please, let's discuss how to frame the wishes involved in each of the items on your list, and then you'll present your generalized but carefully crafted wishes to John, but one at a time, and with a firm finger on the "Undo" button in the event of any unpleasant consequence. Hesitation has conquered continents! Eventually.

SIMON: No ma'am, let's get going! First of all, I'm hungry, and I'll wager you and Simone are, too. *Simon says, let each of us be comfortably filled with nutritious food, over and out.* See, it works! I even feel a happy burp coming up for air!

SIMONE: Why, indeed I do feel my tummy quiescent, and that pleasant lethargy after a leisurely repast! But it just occurred to me, Simon, you know I do miss the repast itself. I like to eat, and by jiminy, so do you. Maybe Yam's insistence on discretion does merit a mullover.

YAM: Good thinking, Miz Elron. Thanks for comin' 'round the hill o' beans. Between the two of us, maybe we can slow down this impetuous spouse of yours, before he careens into blunder. Why rush to wish for unexplored pleasures by foregoing one which, though shamelessly orthodox, is so universally enjoyed that it provides the focus for family and social occasion?

SIMON: Goshahokey, I'm so abashed. Indeed, for speed, what need? Let's calmly address the list, then. Maybe you're right about the "smarts" item. I guess it would be prudent to preserve my own intellectual integrity and delegate the smarts department to you. Temporarily, anyway. What's next?

SIMONE: Item 2): Luxury. Surely there's nothing inappropriate about living in easy swank, eh Yam?

YAM: Well, maybe not. But note that the pleasure derived from "luxury" is generated, in considerable part, through the envy of others. If others are not present, as by your own interdict *is* the case within this citadel, then perhaps "luxury" could get to be downright ugly and uncomfortable. Perhaps "sensual gratification" would be more appropriate? Look, Hepplewhite furnishings and Kandinsky splashes on the wall would be, by any standard, luxurious. Is that what you want?

SIMON: You know I don't. But don't you think my "gentleman's genie" would know that? You're wobbling around now on your "wee wee wee."

SIMONE: All the way home! You blew it this time, Snosnibor.

YAM: Did I? I think that's why John sent me here as an advisor, to avoid the need of his having to decipher what Simon really means from what Simon really says. Kindness and generosity and going-the-extra-mileness cannot be "Simon said." That's not in the agreement. John can look between the lines to interpret intent, but he can't alter what is loudly and clearly stated. Don't push him. He can get very literal if he tires of the game.

SIMONE: Pish-posh, b'gosh. You know Simey dear, we really don't dig *arte moderne*. And this place is comfy, but it could use a little sprucing up. Take care of it, hon.

SIMON: *Simon says, make this place more appealing to the sensibilities of my wife and myself. Over and out.*

YAM: Look, look, over there!

SIMONE: Ooh, la la! This is great! Our favorite *artiste*! An original-looking Hieronymus Bosch hanging over the fireplace! It is real?

SIMON: Does it matter? Looks real enough to me. Only an expert could tell, but as Yam said, by my own fiat an expert can't get in this place. Just we and that choir that follows us around, but they're just flowers on the wall. Now that I think about it, an original would occasion problems for John and me involving possible unpetty larceny. Hey, how about that Mickey Mouse clock on the mantle? It doesn't get any better! What's next on the list, *Simona mia*?

SIMONE: Number 3. It's *amore*! You've already got it, babe. But I know what you mean. You want everybody to think you're a great guy .

YAM: Now, you see, is where you have to think a little more. In the first place, nobody knows you at all. For everybody to think you're a great guy, they've got to have a reason to hang it on. John can handle it, but you might want to think about it first. Do you want to be a great philanthropist? The teacher of the year? A heavy-metal hunk? In any case, you need to build a track record, and allow a network of groupies to emerge and promote you.

SIMON: How about being a grinny overly-Oscared thespian?

YAM: John can get you started in any of those callings, and
              see it through with you, but you realize it takes time.
              Unless you mean you want to assume the body and
              situation of some already-created careerist. That's an
              alternate scene. One that's been dealt with in the
              movies, by the way.

SIMON: Put it on hold. Next item?

SIMONE: Fun! It's about time.

SIMON: Done! *Simon says, let us have a bit of harmless fun, in
              accordance with our notion of the same, over and out.*

JOHN: A masked ball is in progress in Shangri-La. You shall
              join it immediately! Here are your costumes. Don them
              and you are there! Just for fifteen minutes, and then you
              can get on with your to-do list.

CHORUS: Images appear of a boop-a-doop orchestra and
              an enthusiastic crowd surrounding our
              protagonists. The orchestra is playing boop-a-
              doop music, and the crowd is chanting,
              "Dance, dance, Simon and Simone!" Mr. and
              Mrs. Elron put down their glasses of
              champagne, and dance, accompanied by
              applause and appreciative huzzahs from all
              guests. Fifteen minutes pass quickly, and the
              images are gone. Simon and Simone undon
              their apparel.

SIMONE: Wowie! (gasp, gasp) that genie knows what makes us
              tick! I could line up for another ticket on that ride!

SIMON:　　No problem, milady. We can always repeat and improve upon any of this! We're just running through a quickie sampler. Unlimited wish access, remember? What now?

SIMONE:　"Gratification," according to your wishlist.

YAM:　　You mean like the aftermath of a horrible but scratchable itching? I can't imagine anything more gratifying than the relief afforded by a scratched itch.

SIMONE:　You do kid, *madame*. We all know what he means. He's such a conventional euphemizer. Anyhow, I supply all the gratification he needs. You might wish, Don Simon, that it be of unparalleled caliber, always on tap. And of course, that it be mutually gratifying. And that any extracurricular lusting in your heart would provoke something akin to burning your fingers on the stove.

SIMON:　　Can't improve on that. *Simon says, you heard the lady. Just do it. Over and out.* OUCH!... (just kidding).

YAM:　　Hear ye hear ye! Can you in a moment ideate a better satisfaction than what has carefully evolved over millions of years?

SIMONE:　"Fame" is next in line. Advise us, Madam Yam.

YAM:　　My dearest Simone, you are forgetting your role. You and I advise Simon, remember? What is your opinion as to how he should go about wishing to be famous?

SIMONE:　Well, it doesn't seem to be particularly different from the problem of being universally liked. Universally-liked guys are all famous, you know, although not all famous guys are universally liked. Still, the same principle seems to apply here. If Simon's going to be famous, first there's got to be a reason to hang it on, just like you said, Yam. And if you don't feel that you have achieved fame on your own merits, it kind of takes the punch out of it. It's the realization of accomplishment that provides the exhilaration, isn't it? What was our solution to the earlier problem?

SIMON: As I recall, we decided to think that one over. Next in line, please.

SIMONE: *El número siete*: VENGEANCE! Boy can we spend time on this juicy fruit! Remember old Mrs. Corbett in your 8th grade English class? She gave you a "C" just for painting a moustache on the picture of FDR she had on the blackboard. I know just the thing! We'll have John put a bag of *caca* on her front porch, set a match to it, ring the doorbell and skedaddle!

SIMON: That venerable dame (may she RIP) is dead, Simone. And besides, fire's a hazard. I've got it! The guy who put up his house in Manhattan Beach as a prize in an Internet essay contest and then awarded it to himself because the rules didn't say he couldn't! His little trick cost me $400 in entrance fees. John can put the bag of *caca* above his front door, tie it to the doorknob, ring the doorbell, and skedaddle!

YAM: Such tiny-mindedness! Be grateful, rather, to those who advance your wisdom. Now you know that he who expresses contempt for the sacred symbols of those who are paid to judge him, invites a caning. And you have learned to sponsor, not to enter, essay contests on the Internet. This is priceless advice. Why don't you tackle a world-class evil-doer, and forget the silly kid stunts! Take advantage of John's potential. Wreak vengeance on somebody worth the wreaking!

CHORUS: Simon gives it his best shot, but John finds it unclear and advises him to ask his committee ladies, who suggest three prominent evildoers. Simon picks out one and informs John of his choice. Then Yam turns on the TV. Adlai the Glib, Ambassador to the UN from the Blessed States of Vespuccia, is finalizing his sermon to the General Assembly. *"Mene, mene tekel!"* he thunderates, pointing at Belshazzar, the Ayatollah of Babylon. As the General Assemblymen cackle and roar, a scowling Belshazzar assumes the podium and prepares to lecture the sassy Adlai. Suddenly and inexplicably, the Ayatollah moves his head to and fro, stretches his neck, blinks and shouts, *"MENE MENE ##*@!! *#!@!!"* Grunting and barking, he kicks the Secretary General, which so disgraces the Ayatollah in the eyes of the entire world that his one-man government crashes, and is quickly replaced by the shadowy cabal of the underground Papist Party of Mesopotamia, and there is much clinking of chalice in the streets of Babylon. Simon and Simone are cheering at their TV set as these distant events gallop across the screen.

SIMONE: Great show, but I see that John is pandering to Simon's crackpot bent. Why so sensational a solution? Consider Ozma's lowkey remedy for the Growleywog problem. John could have just waved his baton and let Belshazzar *see the light on the road to Damascus*, or something equally less spectacular. No revolution, bloodless or otherwise, just a change of mind. I mean, who cares if the old Belshazzar would or wouldn't recognize the new Belshazzar. He would free all political prisoners and call for immediate free elections!

SIMON: Reasonably cogitated, Simone! We shall democratize the world! Shall we proceed?

YAM: But could the new, idealistic Belshazzar convert the populace? I garland your intent, but do you really want indigent and unlettered varletry electing their governments? Politically correct or not, that hasn't worked out yet. You might consider promoting liberal education, and wait for a generation to be illumined. Maybe then they'll know how to keep illiberal despots off the throne. However, we should be talking about vengeance, not reform.

SIMON: I see, I see. We'll set up a committee to elaborate a white paper on nation-building. Good luck, Babylon. What's eighth on our agenda?

SIMONE: Obeisance, milord. That's mighty important. You don't want folks contradicting you. "Waiter!, the best table, *tout suite*. Get rid of those drunken senators, or whatever they are. NOW!" What deep satisfaction! And then, as we pick our teeth: "You know what you can do with that check, don't you, Mr. *Maître D*'?"

SIMON: A conflict here I see with item number three. We'll have to figure out how to compatabilitize "love me" with "do what I say."

YAM: Any mom can do that. So you can achieve the best table and a free lunch with just a smile and a firm hand. Of course, you'll probably have to forgo whatever enjoyment you might obtain through insulting people and getting away with it. But is that really of importance to you? You did come up with your list without deliberation. Maybe we should revise your list.

SIMONE: It is a Jekyll-Hydeish thing, isn't it? Maybe he could be two guys: Mr. Supersaint on MoWeF, and on TuThSa, Mr. Mother-of-All-Godfathers. That way he could enjoy both sensations and get the goodies at the same time.

SIMON: Sounds schizophrenic and counterproductive. Back-burn it and on to number nine.

SIMONE: Eternal life!

SIMON: We'll waste no time here. That should have been #1. What if we had been struck by lightning while we were fooling around? *Simon says, let me and my wife age no more, let us be impervious to all harm, from whatever source, animal, vegetable or neither animal nor vegetable, over and out.*

YAM: Let me mull aloud a piece. What about your progeny? Shall they, too, live forever? And what about their progeny? And on down the line? Granted, you could wish for more and more food and a bigger and bigger planet, but you realize a continual adjustment of the universe would be necessary just to permit you and your descendents to offend the balance. Or are you prepared to tell your children that you will outlive them? Or that they're off the hook, but that they'll have to so inform their own kids? Don't you see any dilemma here?

SIMON: Maybe we shouldn't have kids at all. Could be they only work for folks who don't live forever? I reckon that's the price we pay.

SIMONE: Simon! What happened to our schemes for Li'l Simon and Li'l Simone? Don't they mean something to both of us quite apart from our living forever? Kids will bind us with mutualness during our eternity. Wow! I feel immortal already! We'll outlive the sun!

SIMON: Oh what a goose I am! Of course you're right, Simone. We'll confound Malthusian doctrine and migrate to other cosmic climes before we get to the twilight of the sun. There's more than one cosmos out there. We'll have John do some scouting. He can even make a universe to order for us and the Simonettes! Number ten, please, while we're waiting, Simone.

YAM: Tra tra-tra! It's .....

SIMONE: Glorification! Hey, St. Simon, maybe this is a bit much. Possible bighead side effects? Or maybe John will decide you want to be chunk of holy marble in the Vatican? Go ahead and try it on for size if you must, but this hand, deal me out.

YAM: Need I say we'd better think this one through? Or do you already have it figured out?

SIMON: I figured that the first thing you'd say is that I don't really need it or want it. But as a matter of fact, I do want it and I do need it. It's just a next logical step from the "Goody-Two-Sandal Gandhi" scenario. You know the problems movie stars have with pesterazzi? Well, canonization puts us on a pedestal above botheration! There are still some kookaburras who will be shooting at us, but they don't abound, and won't be any more of a nuisance than an occasional gnat, impervious as we are to lethal attack. Being sanctified is, you see, a sound investment in privacy, which in the flashy light of our superstardom we will require. When we amble in the park it will be far preferable for folks to prostrate themselves and grovel, rather than for them to rush up, gush, and demand an autograph.

YAM: You build a practical case for sainthood, my son. But don't let it get to your noggin. And on that subject, we can accomplish the same feeling of self importance just by punching the right buttons in your brain, without your ambling anywhere.

SIMON: Your alternative smacks of eating hashish. Ambling in the park is somehow more appealing to simple Simon, who digs the crisp crack of five-sense reality. No buttons, *madame*. How about some exalted reality! *Simon says, let me be glorified above all men! Over and out.*

CHORUS: Yam falls on her face. The sun goes out, or maybe not. The Exalted One seems to gleam with holy innerfire. John appears and genuflects.

JOHN: *Inshaalha.* So be it, Most Glorious Master!

SIMON: Holy Moley, look at the clock! It's 'way past bedtime. Simone, don't even think about wishing us to be sleepless robots. I pity the wide-eyed Tin Woodman that only stands and waits.

SIMONE: Yea, we've plenty of time. What would we do while our comrades are in Nodland? Watch infomercials? Excuse us, Yam. You can sleep on the rug, if John can't put you up in Genielandia.

YAM: Before you retire, O Sanctified Celestial, let John amaze you with the awesome legerdemain he's been saving up his sleeve for you. Make his day! It'll mean so much to him.

SIMON: Well, that's the least we can do to show a spot of gratitude. *Simon says, let's see an awesome magic trick! Over and out.*

JOHN: Exalted Superseraph, I never thought thou'd ask. Behold! I can turn a dusty old useless manuscript into a rabbit. Dost thou happen to have a yellowed scroll handy?

SIMON: Well, there's this ancient scroll I picked up at the Goodwill. I have it hidden here behind a brick in the fireplace. I haven't had a chance to check it out. Hey, you can translate it b'gosh! Even Old Macdonald didn't know what it was. Ake-shay a eg-lay!

(chuckle).That's pig-Latin, John, ig-pay atin-Lay. An improved version of Esperanto I picked up at Okefenokee U. I'll explain it to you ater-lay. Now, on with your stunt.

JOHN: Not to worry! Hand over the scroll, O Master of the Firmament. Thy mouth shall gape.

SIMON: Holy Hare O' Jack! A gray rabbit in its stead! I've seen it all! OK, now change it back into my scroll and reveal to all its significance.

JOHN: Presto Digitato! Here it is again. It's a recipe for camel's hair soup, transliterated from an obscure Shishkabob dialect. Could bring you ten big bucks on eBay.

SIMONE: May I check that scroll please, sir? Aha! Just what I was fishing for! You've entrapped yourselves into a felony, folks. Don't make a move, you two. This little heater is not a prop that shoots a "BANG" banner. And this is not the scroll Simon handed you. The old switcheroo! Stick the camel soup back up your sleeve and hand over the real scroll. I can see it sticking out from here, you fool. Don't bother with any more tricks this evening... this is it, all right: OMODOQUAY ITTERAELAY ELIGIOSAERAY IISPAY CRIBERESAY, A ANCTOSAY OANNEIAY.

SIMON: What th'! Simone, why th', who th', where th'? Tell me you're legpulling! Squeeze the trigger and let the "BANG" banner appear!

SIMONE: Sorry your magic carpet just ran out of petrol, mate.

Clouds, disperse! What an afterclap, eh Simon? These humbugs were going to alakazam outa here along with your priceless scroll! It's the first "How-To" manual ever scripted, St. John's *How To Write Gospels for Gullibles*. Valued at many shekels! It languished unsung for centuries in the used wallpaper section of Goodwill Industries. Simon was the first to suspect that it was not used wallpaper at all! From the gitgo, Yam's constant stalling signaled phonaloney. But I bided, I did, and played the game. As for the apparently fulfilled wishes, most were either parlor tricks, or simply suggestion, unverifiable until too-late time. And it didn't take tea leaves to divine what direction these wishes would probably take.

YAM: Dissembler! Agitator! Agnostic! How about the Bosch original and the Mickey Mouse clock! That was *sortilège!*

SIMONE: Ha! Remember when you spent so long in the bathroom? You were dyeing John's gossamer handkerchiefs the color of our wall! Then you attached black threads to them and took those junky items from your purse, draped the tinted hankies over them, and surreptitiously put them in their places. When you pronounced "Lo!" you simply jerked the threads and palmed the hankies while we were gawking at our newly acquired art. The Bosch is just a calendar print, by the way. Dissembler yourself! Yam's a sham!

SIMON: But how did they make you magically appear in the store?

SIMONE: Pshaw. Yam saw me coming into the store and told you to wish for me.

JOHN: Thou canst not be serious. How explainest thou the miraculous trip to Shangri-La? The overthrow of the Ayatollah Belshazzar?

SIMONE: Shangri-La? Virtual-Reality gadgetry. Why a *masked* ball? So we wouldn't suspect that those awkward masks we had to put on were really V-R goggles. As for the Ayatollah, you had three tapes prepared with identical scenarios, but each with a different "Axis of Evil" villain portrayed, to document the real-time overthrow of their evil regime. This stunt didn't exactly qualify as "vengeance," but you convinced us that it did. Of course, Yam suggested three names, and slipped the tape that Simon selected into the VCR as she turned on the TV. And you can cut the funny talk, Macdonald, and take off your turban and the fake nose. I couldn't figure out what you were after until you asked for the scroll. Suddenly Simon's casual pig-Latin aside aha'd inside my head, and the last chink clinked into its niche! The scroll was written in pig-Latin Latin! When Simon asked you if you recognized the language, he had hidden the scroll and only showed you the title he had copied to a Post-It. During the War, you served as head of the Pig-Latin Division of the OSS. At some point you recognized the pig-Latin Latin, and understood the significance of the title. Simon bristled at your suggestion that he might have made a mistake in copying the title of the manuscript, and demurred when you requested to see the original document. You immediately began to scheme to pilfer the scroll. You recruited two of your drinkin' buddies at the *Hungry I* as abettors, one to wrap himself in your greatcoat and impersonate you at the store, and the other, of course, is our dear petite Yam, and together you concocted this amusing hoax.

SIMON: Old Mac, *traditore*! I had a glimmer, I did, that the bubble would pop, but my crazy id just couldn't let that notion prosper. No wonder you knew so much about us! But ha ha ha, John Genie, AKA Macdonald, your pulling multi-colored hankies from my nose hardly fooled me at all. Damn! Back to the nine-to-five rut.

SIMONE: The jig is over, it's the jug for you two for pettifoggery! Arrest them, Sergeant Hezzie!

CHORUS: An SFPD sergeant, disguised as one of our countertenors, breaks from our ranks and handcuffs the miscreants.

HEZZIE: *LA COMMEDIA E FINITA.*

JOHN: Curses! Foiled by a pair of nerdy Babbitts!

SIMON: Have you no shame, Old Macdonald? You can while away the years cozening your fellow losers on Devil's Island, Mister Kerplunk Yerout! March them off to the hoosegow, *gendarme*.

SIMONE: Heigh-ho, heigh-ho, Yam-In-A-Jam, away-you-go, alakazam, ma'am!

YAM: Ah, the fanfaronade of the victor! Say what you may; the advice I impart is *recherché*. One final injunction: do not discard my counsel. It's of more benefit to you than the wishes might have been.

SIMON: What do you want? The last *bon mot*? Not on your twirlytoe, ho, ho, ho. Scram, Yam! Dearest Simone, this scroll is a blessed event! I can now complete my work, *Bionosis, the Art of Auto-Delusion*. I'll putsch ol' Potter off the pedestal and terrorize the bestseller list for a thousand years. Read the *Great Books of the Western World*? I'll WRITE 'em! Simon Elron will be a Major Prophet! Wealthy! Worshipped! Have fun! Live forever vicariously through his never-O.P. opuses! What defter tutor to have at my elbow than St. John the Divine. The scroll is worth more for my eyes alone than for whatever pittance it might pull on the auction block. And now, lucky Simon, to bed. With your snuggly Simone. Really, can any geniewish top that?

Editor's note: As this book was to hit the press, boggling news regarding the fate of Yam Snosnibor appeared on the Clootie Channel. Turn page for bombshell event.

☞

(Transcript of the Harry Clootie Interview with Yam Snosnibor on the steps of the Stanislaus County Jail, where she was released after a trial that acquitted her of all charges.)

CLOOTIE: I'LL BE AN AVUNCULAR MONKEY! You DID IT! And they're acquitting Big Mac right now! No one would have given TUPPENCE for your chances two months ago, but now you're out and ON THE CIRCUIT! Tell inquiring fans: how did you BEAT THE SYSTEM?

SNOSNIBOR: Elementary stuff, my dear inquirers. No need for any moneypit shyster. I appointed myself counsel, and took on a Boalt Hall fresher working for busfare to sit by me and tell me when to object. We hired the Pettifog Jurystacking Service and profiled my most favorable juror. We demanded a change of venue until we found one teeming with stereotypes. I wrote and delivered a rousing preamble and epilogue. *Voilà!* Justice is served.

CLOOTIE: Make mine MEDIUM RARE! You know, your defense based on deference to the Laws of a HIGHER POWER in keeping SACRED SCRIPTURE from the sullied hands of Simon Elron, alleged CLOSET SCOFFJESUS, really RANG A DING-DONG with these Stanislaus fundamentalists. Your summation was SOOO COOL: "God said it, you believe it, end of trial!" Then, when you led the jury in a rousing Hallelujah Chorus, that was AWESOME!

SNOSNIBOR: My blushes, Clootie-pie. And in the by-and-by, I'll see you ... at the *Hungry I*!"

... just so long will genius please the talentgang

By definition, geniuses are eccentric. Some folks even maintain that there is a touch of madness in genius, and they trot out a list of stereotypes. "Lefty" Scaevola is the name that invariably heads these lists. The world didn't know what to do with "Lefty," but he had definite ideas about what to do with the world. However, his healthy selfesteem afforded little margin for diplomacy, and attentiongetting shenanigans to promote his plan to redeem the planet only irritated those already in charge of running the world.

... just so long will genius please the talentgang

a twoacter, including a prologue and an epilogue, and a title and a *denouement* by ee cummings

cast of characters

chorus *volunteers from audience (please arrive tenminutes early)*
reddy milliwit *techsupport supervisor*
asar alubat *behaviourist communicant, advisor to senator hillaham*
three mesamorphs *international negotiators*
denise lamenace *honorstudent at peekachoo academy*
lefty scaevola *dogooder genius on attorneygenerals list*
special inquisitor *grand prosecutor*
arry th angman *selfstyled stylish cockney*

**PROLOGUE: A subway car en route to Rockefeller Center.
Reddy Milliwit, Asar Alubat, three international negotiators,
Denise Lamenace, Chorus.**

CHORUS: Dr. "Lefty" Scaevola, operating from some inaccessible hideaway, holds the whole e-world in his left hand. He and his organization, "The Mystic Nits of the Internet," have announced to the world through their "Manifesto" that they possess the only copy of the Great Backup Disk, on which the welfare of the entire world.com depends. He and his crew of brilliantly twisted minds, having infiltrated every major computer center in the world, have been able to destroy all other Great Backup copies, and have invited world leaders to send a task force to meet with Scaevola in order to

discuss alternatives to the destruction of the only remaining Great Backup Disk.

According to the Manifesto, this would involve the establishment of the "Select People's Quorum Reglamentarians" composed of particularly clever Mystic Nits appointed by the de facto Chairman, "Lefty" Scaevola himself. A secret meeting has been arranged in Rockefeller Center. Task force members representing the civilized world.com are instructed to come with giant floating Betty Boop party balloons so they can easily be spotted in the crowd. Scaevola himself will be disguised. Reddy Milliwit, team *kahuna* cloaked with Greater Good, has preemptively informed the FBI of the secret meeting; so the Feds, too, will be watching the balloons, ready to pounce on Scaevola when he approaches to make contact.

MILLIWIT: Man, this Scaevola is some Odd Johnson! Go-go genius, maybe, but for me, a real banshee. If it weren't for his own private "Nestorian Project" that has heads of state abuzz, I'd say snuff the buzzard. We can still recreate a new Great Backup, according to contract-hungry oracles. Of course, it would be tricky, and too late in case of another crash or unforeimagined glitch. I shudder to think of the collapse of e-chat if we don't succeed. Millions will flock to the call of Armageddon-eyed evangelists and disrupt e-commerce. NASDAQ would close its e-doors, and I'd be out of an e-job! He's The e-Man when it comes to hacking.com. And in my salad days he was such a hero! What did you learn about his murky past, Asar?

ALUBAT: Grab your *sombrero*, Reddy. The psychodossier we
compiled on this ectomorph is spellbinding. Since
grammar school he was a cut above Terman's capacity
to quantify. Before he was in the first grade, he had
invented a scientific variant of TicTacToe. Instead of
X's and O's he used Xe's and O^2's! In high school, he
was a wonderful whiz. He was ever an all A achiever,
except for a painful C in Trigonometry. Seems that he
found the final so absurdly simple that he couldn't
refrain from chortling the entire period, which made his
eyes water so that he couldn't see the last two problems!
He built a robot lookalike to go to college for him and
get his Ph.D. in CompuSpeak, while he set up his
international network of Mystic Nits. They
communicate all over the world in indecipherable
gestalt codes, consternating your CIA's crack
cryptographists. One code turned out to be a mutation
of pig Latin! Except, instead of "ay" each word ended
with "ee." Thus, "igpee Atinlee!" So simple, it eluded
bureaucratic intelligence for years. Then, when they
were on the verge of discovery, he changed it to end in
"oy" instead of "ee." Back to square *uno* for the CI
agents. Your guys finally cracked the code yesterday, a
day too late, it seems. This is one cleverly deceptive
onsoy-of-a-itchboy!

MILLIWIT: Boy, howdy! And I remember back when we erected a
statue in our town plaza to this guy! You remember,
when he thrust his right hand into a federal courtroom
brazier, protesting big bully governments who bully
little bully wannabes! "Lefty" was our shiny knight!

ALUBAT: And two years later the shine was gone, and the whole
town huzzah'd when you valiently led the posse to blast

away that image in the plaza! *Sic transit gloria.* But here's our stop: Rockefeller Center, Scaevola, and the future of Western Civilization.com as we know it!

CHORUS: As the scheming negotiators debark with their balloons at the Rockefeller Center Station, they are intercepted by a goateed stranger with a Cat-In-The-Hat hat, who hands Milliwit a menacing broadside which asserts that if they ever expect to see the Great Backup in useable condition, they had best shutup and follow the stranger's behest. The stranger then orders the dismayed negotiators to hand over their balloons to a girl scout troop passing by on a tour of Rockefeller Plaza. He instructs Milliwit & Co. to march to the Empire State Building, where they take the elevator to the top. Little Denise whispers to Milliwit that the right coat sleeve of their kidnapper seems to be pinned to the coat pocket. Milliwit and Alubat exchange amazed glances. The mysterious stranger, looking more and more like "Lefty" Scaevola, hands the floor security guy a bag of gold, of recent vintage. He then commands this new recruit to chase the tourists out of the observation platform and stand guard at the door until the meeting is adjourned. Scaevola, for apparently it *is* he, removes his goatee and sets up shop. Back at Rockefeller Center, the hoodwinked FBI agents are stalking the Campfire Girls with the saucy Betty Boop balloons bobbing above the mob.

ACT I -- . Empire State Bldg. observation platform, noontime.
Scaevola, Milliwit, Alubat, Denise Lamenace (a rose
in her hand), three international negotiators, chorus.

CHORUS: What does Dr. Scaevola mean when he says
            man has failed to live up to Nature's
            Expectations? Why does he say we have sold
            our birthright in exchange for voluntary
            servitude to evanescent gadgets and fatass
            politicos? What is this mysterious machine that
            stands before him, with his hand resting on its
            menacing lever, and where did it come from?
            Will we never know the answer to these
            nagging enigmas?

SCAEVOLA: Hail, negotiating eggnoggins! Now in peace we can
            parley. I see amazement writ on your crockpates. You
            are wondering how I got to the subway station, through
            your pathetic security checks, with this apparatus. Well,
            I wore a fake goatee, and the machine was under my
            roomy Cat-In-The-Hat hat. Fools! Were you expecting
            an apocalypic device? *Pulgas, con bombas atómicas no
            matarás.* Right, *Señor* Alubat? The machine is just a
            citrus juicer, but you will note that instead of a lemon
            in its maw there is a shiny disk -- the only remaining
            Great Backup! I push the lever and the disk is rendered
            useless. You'll never put together again its mangled bits
            'n' bytes! On the other hand, if you accept the terms of
            my Manifesto, as appearing in last month's *Hustler*, you
            get your disk back and we will proceed to dismantle
            world hogtroughocracy at a temperate pace, steadily
            transferring hegemony to the Reglamentarians. Eons
            past, the ancient ones built compasses into our psyche,
            but they are smogged up and flatlining, and your luck in

blundering into survival in spite of yourselves will fizzle. Our Mystic Nit benevolent technocracy will link economy and government to the principles of the ancient bearded ones. Back to the generative powers of creation! I, "Lefty" Scaevola, will the New Messiah be, the Prophet of Deuteronomy! Ye shall hearken, simpletons, unto me! What say ye?

MILLIWIT: Look, Scaevola, we printed your Manifesto. We are prepared to send it to a really serious Senate subcommittee for bipartisan mulling. We can set it up so you can testify before this committee, and grant you considerable immunity in exchange for your collaboration. We will even print your picture on the cover of Time magazine! Just give us back our Great Backup and rejoin our commonsense society. You can continue to work on your Nestorian Project, of course with appropriate congressional oversight. If it ever works, or even if it doesn't, we'll see that you get a Slap-on-the-Back letter from the Prez himself. We do expect you to turn over to the FBI a list with the names of all the members of the Mystic Nits of the Internet.

SCAEVOLA: Hee, hee, hee! Chortle, chortle, (on and on).....

ALUBAT: Think of something sad, "Lefty", so we can continue. Remember Ed Wynn's gig in "Mary Poppins?" If you had known that trick when you were taking your Trig exam, you'd have been able to see the last two problems. As it is, you will always have a smirch on your career.

SCAEVOLA: (no longer chortling, as he thinks angrily of the smirch) My jealously insane Trig instructor set the trap for me

by elaborating a final exam worthy of charlienoodles.
He deliberately provoked my manic hilarity. But forget
not, Mr., as it were, Megapoop, I have the hand that's
upper and the lip that's stiff.

MILLIWIT: (bluffing) Let me tell you, Dr. -- in what? Bionosis?
Whatever. Dr. Scroobola, you have shortsold your
plodding adversaries. We are on the verge of recreating
the Great Backup disk!

SCAEVOLA: On the verge of hoohah! You miserable muggles will
never deal fast enough to trump my aces! Hear ye, hear
ye: on every hard disk in the world ever connected to
the Internet, there is a timebomb cookie, which will
explode in "x" minutes, and wreak unheard-of calamity
unless I give word to my Mystic Nit cohorts to make
available the quickie download fix. Just say "uncle!"
and I greenlight the antidote, like jiffyquick.

DENISE: (nudged by Alubat, proffers her rose) Please sir, accept
this flower as testimony to the innocence of children,
and our total dependence on guilty adults.

SCAEVOLA: Do I look like a sucker, kid? Give me that rose, so I can
shove it up Alubat's nose!

CHORUS: As he reaches for the rose, he takes his hand
off the lever, and the three silent negotiators,
who in fact are judo pros who had carefully
rehearsed this moment, leap at the hapless
hacker and in a blinky twist pin him to the
concrete. Alubat produces a rope -- cleverly
concealed somewhere on his humanity -- and

with Milliwit's help, the outnumbered terrorist
is hogtied.

DENISE: (pushing down on the lever, crushing the Great Backup)
What's this?

**ACT II --   The International Inquisition, somewhere in *Tierra del
Fuego*. Special Inquisitor, Scaevola, chorus.**

INQUISITOR: Hear ye, hear ye; come to order, ye. Bailiff, remove
the court braziers, we'll have no fiery histrionics here. I
was just reading in the Daily Breeze about this case,
and I must say, I am appalled. Especially compelling
was the Oliphant cartoon. As of two weeks ago, since
the cookie explosion, the entire Internet consists only of
Scaevola's Manifesto. I can't imagine how the
defendant could possibly argufy himself out of this, but
who am I to judge? So say away, culprit Scaevola.

SCAEVOLA: Ye've got the wrong perp, ye twerp. The Great Backup
was destroyed, albeit witlessly, by an out-of-control
brat, not by me. I was prepared to deal, and you guys let
a spongideformed Skinnerian devise a scheme which
screwed up everything. The Great Backup, smashed;
the cookie timebomb, detonated; me, on trial. And you
can just forget about the Nestorian Project, not to
mention any other contribution to humanity a man of
my genius could conceivably come up with.

INQUISITOR: Don't worry about your Nestoriana, Scaevola. It's
historical poop! Congressional Special Abettor Dr.
Billy Brutus, D.D., Litt. D., has looked at it, and has
just denounced it as yet another phantastical search for

the Philosopher's Stone. Ye pretend to silently morph any atom into any other atom -- imagine that! Dr. Brutus has concluded that ye have really rocked off yer horsie. He states that, with yer rantings, ye are more of an abomination than Spiro Agnew! So ye see, ye are expendable, and unless I seriously underestimate the commitment of the jury to the tenets of legal fiat, ye will be swatted like a stinkbug. They tell me it will take weeks before yer Manifesto is purged from the Internet. Is this the only way ye could get anybody to read it? That, sirrah, is heinous and a half. I shudder to contemplate what new and grimmer hoax a liberated Scaevola would come up with as a prescription fer perceived transgressions, and at what catastrophic cost. In any event, we men in black are enjoined to punish the heinous, not to determine their potential utility in spite of their heinousness.

SCAEVOLA: I am being judged by simpletons, as were Socrates and Cagliostro before me! Brutus is a poohbah consumed with pomp. He would hang Isaac Newton to the sour apple tree had he the time machine to do it. I have dedicated my energies to reconstruct what was learned and lost many generations past, but which did lead us to the where we are. I have penetrated to great depth the tunnel of new technology and have perceived gloom. While the wisdom of the ancients abides in the stars, you entrust systems of wind and sand to record your own knowledge. You have stashed it all in attic of the Library of Ozymandias. Don't you grasp that the survival of the human race depends on the General Theory of the Philosopher's Stone? The alchemists were on to something, and I'm at the brink of cracking that nut. Without me and my Nestorian studies you are doomed. You and your history -- poop and all! -- will disappear.

INQUISITOR: Tomorrow takes care of herself, Dr. Cock-a-doodle-doo. Methinks ye have problems in yer perspective. Has yer self-implanted crown of thorns allowed blood to trickle into yer eyes and color the scenery? Were ye to go free, license would be issued to each and every zany with a bent to save the world with wee regard for environmental impact. While ye may be the only loon in the lagoon who could conceivably hector the world to its kneecaps, still the idea of a mob of would-be saviors with their heads full of parables and their hands on doomsday levers is, at the least, latent with nuisance. Perhaps the fact that the execution of the Grandee of Galilee provided an impetus to His movement can cheer ye on yer way to the scaffold. Some day they may name a church after ye, but ye'll not prosper on my watch, ye nut. I've got me marching orders, and so, heigh-ho heigh-ho, to the gallows ye go.

SCAEVOLA: There's no point in my coming up with any famous last *mots*. You're such nincomnattering nudniks that you couldn't figure them out, anyway. You will always see sorcerers in your scientists, Machiavellis in your Messiahs. You have heeded the croaking of Billy Brutus, and may you all fall into a big black hole.

CHORUS: The Special Inquisitor hurls the Book of Charges at Scaevola, knocking him, ingloriously, down. He then wakes the jury, and in harmony they mumble, "You're guilty! Guilty! Guilty!" The Inquisitor intones, "The gibbet! Gibbet! Gibbet!"

EPILOGUE --   **A plain with a gallows, early morning. Scaevola, 'arry the 'angman, chorus.**

CHORUS: The birds are singing, but not for Scaevola. He marches to the scaffolding conveniently placed on a little hill so all can see without shoving. On a civil obedience fieldtrip, Mrs. Defarge's U.S. History class from Peekachoo Academy is lined up in the front row. Some of the kids are sporting Betty Boop balloons, with the teenybop head, touseled do, pizza-pie eyes and streetwise attitude, pertly bobbing above the multitude. Scaevola has something in his hand that all mistake for a Kleenex. There is no sound, until the hangman, underwhelmed by the glory of his fifteen minutes, farts. The crowd gasps. And now the noose is placed around Scaevola's neck! And now the trapdoor lever is pushed! And now the hush is smashed by the clatter of metal on wood! "Scaevola" is a roboScaevola!   His robohead clunks down the steps of the scaffold, boop, boop, boop, boop-a-doop, and rolls down the hill.

'ARRY: Blimey, h'odds bodkins! H'it's a bloody robot! An' what's this 'ere, h'in 'is blinkin' 'and? H'it's no bloody nosewiper, h'it's a bloomin' Las' Will an' Testyment! H'it sez:

            Look h'up h'in th' sky, that streak y' see h'isn't h'ay NASER shot, h'it's h'I, th' real "Lefty" Scaevoler, an' th' loverly Princess Layer, an' me functionin' Philoserfer's Stone, leavin' jetspray h'in yer face. We're 'eaded fer h'Arctoorus, where th' h'air h'is h'unpolluted (we'll make h'it that way) th' water tastes like Liebfraumilch *an' th' climate suits yer fineree   (h'it's h'ever h'ay day h'in May)! So go take h'ay sink h'in th' drink with Brootus, D.D. See yez (not vurry likely, h'if yez don' figger h'it h'out)! But th' loverly Layer an' h'I, we'll do yez proud, with h'ay new 'uman race o' pretty smarties! Maybe ye'll take h'ay gander now h'at me Mannyfesto, an' support yer local Mystic Nits, simpletoons! Figger h'it h'out!*

CHORUS: A voice in the crowd cries, "Look up, there's a streak of light headed straight for Arcturus! It's the Enlightened One with his lovely princess! I was blinkered and now I panavisualize! Yea, I have figured it out! Hail to the Mystic Nits and the Philosopher's Stone!" Some murmurs of "Yea!" rumble through the crowd. The inspired converts silently slip away. Escaping the grasp of civically spirited but flabbergasted young fingers, the Betty Boop balloons are chasing after the Arcturus-bound spaceship. The remaining witnesses-to-history are confused, and civil unrest reigns for a time. Then, gathering together in groups of threes and twos, the benighted lookieloos finally go home to check the Evening News, and find out from the Voices-We-Trust just what in blazes this was all about. And you know what? The real "Lefty" Scaevola is probably not even a "Lefty" at all.

... and just so long will being pay the rent of seem

The Excelsior Odyssey

In the history of man's stewardship over all things bright and terrible on his planet, greed, destruction, and self-indulgence have left the once verdant and vibrant jewel of the heavens a shell of its former majesty. There is that story of the man in a far country who earned the wrath of his Master by failing to profit from the sum entrusted to him. At least the sum was returned intact; such has not been the case with the devastated planet earth. The only solution for the animal who permanently soils his den is to find another one; assuming, of course, that another is available. You are about to read the chronicle of a crew on this mission, the tribulation they encountered, and some rather disturbing reverberations from the stone of Sisyphus.

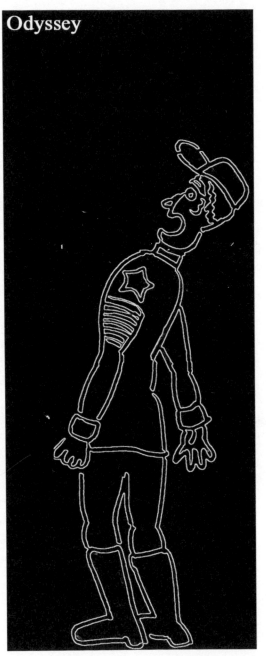

THE EXCELSIOR ODYSSEY

A VOYAGE INTO COSMOGONY

CAST OF CHARACTERS:

LT. ATOM SNURL, FIRST MATE OF THE EXCELSIOR

EVA SNARCESOR, FAST MAID OF THE EXCELSIOR

CAP'N GUNDAR, CAP'N OF THE HOT-SHOT

PETTY OFFICER GRUNCH, OUT-TO-LUNCH COP

CAP'N JICK, CAP'N OF THE EXCELSIOR

KING MOUTH, DECLAMATORY MORTAL INSTRUMENT

MR. VICI, TROUBLOUS MULTIMIND

ROLLING CAPTIONS

BADBITERS

MORTAL INSTRUMENTS

Prologue. Aboard the spaceship *Excelsior*, shot from the
Victorious Emigration Navigation Institute (VENI) outpost on
the planet Mars, at Sea of a Great Leap for a Man.

CAPTIONS: The blackbox nestled in Universe Alpha has
just absorbed its third ergbolt. One more hit
and Blackbox Alpha and its citizens will poof
off to oblivion. Cap'n Alpha, under boggling
pressure, nonetheless has an easy decision:
use the available hypercapacitance to
maneuver strategically the blackbox away
from the violated area. This is not the moment
for offensive action; only two hits have been
scored on the enemy blackbox in Universe
Beta, and there is no clear clue as to its

current position, but Cap'n Beta is both merciless and lucky. Of his following three ergbolts, one hits its target, and Alpha's city-inside-a-cube is silently annihilated: Universe Alpha is empty. Beta is victorious.

Actually, this Ergbolt-the-Blackbox endgame sequence is just a brief verbal joust between Cap'n Jick and Lt. Atom Snurl, two crew members of the Victorious Ship *Excelsior*, en route to Arcturus. In this case, the position of Alpha's blackbox (a 4x4x4 cube) was initially at (2,4,5) -- "position" defined as the vertex nearest the origin of the 10x10x10 coordinate system which comprises a Universe. This was the spoken exchange between Jick and Snurl:

Cap'n Jick, shooting three shots for Cap'n Beta: "(2,9,6); (3,3,7); (4,6,6)."
Lt. Snurl, adjusting position for Cap'n Alpha: "One hit, Cap'n. Repositioning" -- written down but unannounced moves:
(3,4,5); (3,5,5); (4,5,5).
Cap'n Jick: "(3,9,6); (4,3,7); (5,6,6)."
Lt. Snurl: "You poofed me!" Jick's final shot of each volley had scored a hit. Snurl's attempt to maneuver out of range had accomplished zip.

Universes Alpha and Beta are in the mind of the players; positions and shots fired are written down for postgame accounting. Excitement, anticipation, euphoria of victory and ignominy of defeat, all in the heads of Lt.

Snurl and Cap'n Jick.

During the on and on timesilence of cosmonautical life, earthclocks are used to simulate calendar days and weeks, and a specific program is assigned for each day. The work schedule consists of exercise, gastrointestinal duties, cleanup, and readiness drill. After work, time is dedicated to R&R activity. For the first year, the program did not vary. On Mondays, there were Yo-Yo tournaments; Tuesdays were for Ergbolt-the-Blackbox mindgames; Wednesdays, the Megapiece Jigsaw task; Thursdays were spent on the Palindrome Stretch event; Fridays were for Moviewatching. Saturday was devoted to Proving that if the Bisectors of Two Angles of a Triangle are Equal, the Triangle is Isosceles; and Sunday, appropriately or not, was scheduled for Spiritual Meditation. No games involving playing cards or dice had been permitted aboard the *Excelsior* by direct orders of the righteous VENI commissioner, who considered these to be instruments of turpitude. However, after the first year, Cap'n Jick complained of a toothache, and a die was fashioned from the molar that was removed from his troubled jaw. This die permits the R & R activity from Monday through Saturday to be randomly selected, adding a welcome element of suspense to the daily routine. The die is used for no other purpose.

When Lt. Snurl, Cap'n Jick and Eva Snarcesor were shot into hyperspace from the Mars VENI station, smart money said they had a reasonable shot at a successful expedition to Arcturus, in spite of four previous debacles. Leaks from the top-hush *Victorious Intelligence Decipherers Institute* (VIDI) revealed that *Top-Speed, Out-to-Lunch, Lightnin' Bug,* and *Hot-Shot* had shamelessly crashed into Pluto, not even halfway to their destination. However, these were all space projects of previous administrations, and as centuries of environmental abuse were turning the earth into a smoggy marsh, throwing in the towel was not an option. A new spin was the order of the hour; most agreed that *Excelsior* sounded like a nobler name, and new biotechnology now enabled *Excelsior* to be efficiently powered by human body excretions instead of polluting gamma rays. And, too, bumbling old VENI Commissioner "Unprincipled Peter" McCrock was removed from office for making inappropriate advances to a Martian rock. The political community was confident that the efforts to colonize new frontiers would be more successful under the leadership of the new commissioner, Goneril "Nonsense-Stops-Here" O'Nuker, a tough sister. *To seek a newer world, 'tis not too late; smite the sounding furrows!* she was fond of parroting.

And BOOM! Comets and stars are shooting past the *Excelsior* as she smites the cosmic dust! The novelty wears off after a few years, but when Pluto looms large in the ethershield, Lt. Snurl barely has time to announce, "Fasten your seat belts!" and there is a loud noise and an eyeshutting flash.

Act I. A plain on Pluto. It is winter, and colder than a witch's wiggle. Snurl is pulling himself out of the smoking wreck.

SNURL: Eva! Art thou alive and well? Pinioned under a polybutylene crossbeam art thou, whilst the ship about thee burns? Art thou dead-a-ready? *(O my thoughts, dwell rather on the droll!)*

EVA: Peek-a-boo, Snurl, a bad weed keeps growin' and growin'! Embrace weedy ol' needy me, you fool. Are we on Pluto's icy plains? Where is Cap'n Jick? I don't see him anywhere. Guess he didn' make it. If marooned I'm to be on Pluto with thee, Snurl, Jick's-a-crowd.

SNURL: What a lucky stroke; thou, in one piece, Eva! But a real martyr is Jick, by dozing engineers victimized! Into Pluto, why can't they keep us from running? It's a planet, but a big planet it isn't. Emerges a pattern, methinks. What th'! Heads up, Eva! Over there with a zapp gun there's a creature! Hit the ice! *(Through a hoop you leap, no time for high-fives; in your face another hoop!)*

EVA: Hear the fearful zapp-a-dapp, see the om'nous flames an' smoke! We are unhit, but don't fall into that pit that gapes 'twixt us an' that outlander yonder.

SNURL: You, there! In your contemptible mindset is their something amiss, sir? Upon innocent tourists why do you fire, and in such furtive wise? Identify yourself, if with Anglojabber you are conversant! What is your name, rank, and sexual preference? *(An innocuous query will the unwitting lull, and the data base beans will spill!)*

GUNDAR: Holy smoke, now that I've got good gander, you must be Lt. Snurl, of *Excelsior*! Hey, it was just warning shot. Sorry about gaping pit. I'll bet you can't guess who am I. Here's clue for you! My favorite color is pink. Down to life's lees (chugalug) I drink!

SNURL: Why, it's Cap'n "Pinkeye" Gundar, of the ill-fated *Hot-Shot*! Flash of realization notwithstanding, mine own eyes I disbelieve! Explanation is overdue. We have conversation to make! *(In my head a hobgoblin spewing incredulity!)*

GUNDAR: There will be time for chat, Snurl. Most of us bailed out in time. I will take you to nearby crater habitat, where you will meet fellow survivors. You will have bowl of hot soup at Officers' Club. You too, luscious Eva Snarcesor. It's always ladies' night at Club. Hey, where's Jick?

SNURL: That selfless Cap'n went down with his ship, Cap'n Gundar. But he would be happy to know we all remember him fondly. For the invite, thanks. *(A spot o' soup the spot it hits!)*

EVA: (As in silence we follow Gundar, in my head a whisperin' imp: *"Trust not the oglin' slyboots."* In secret code I mutter to Snurl, "undarGay's a akerfay an' a echerlay." He nods and quickly claps a hand over his mouth, eyes achuckle. I silently guffaw. Gundar fools no one!)

GUNDAR: Here we are, your new abode. I open secret door in side of crater. After you....... SUCKERS. I slam secret door! Ha, ha, I have you now! *Hasta la visita, mamacita!*

Act II. A dark cavern in Pluto's bowels.

EVA: Oh me oh my, but herein is dark! What could we else do, Snurl? If we say no, we won't go, then he knows that we know! No way th' clever Cap'n to deceive! Throw yourself with useless vigor at the stubborn door, Snurl!

SNURL: ...Ugh! Between a hard rock and a bad scene, pardner! Trapped are we in the caverns of Pluto at the mercy of the tortfeasing Cap'n Gundar! Officers' Club, Ladies' Night, hot soup, HAW!

EVA: Of us we are two, Snurl; of him there is but one. We have great advan'age.

SNURL: But what is this? Hark to the groan in the corner! Methinks we are unalone! What th'?! My zapp gun's absent! Worthy adversary, Cap'n Gundar! He's heisted me hackbut, and unarmed are we in clearly present danger!

EVA: Feel aroun' at y'r feet, Lieut. There are rocks all aroun' us. They were good enough for Li'l David.

GRUNCH: Lt. Snurl (gasp) it is I, Petty Officer Grunch, of the ill-starred *Out-to-Lunch,* as ever, centered in the sphere of common duties. Here in the corner, sir, waiting (groan) for a chance to speak.

SNURL: Petty-O Grunch! So verities with fibs did Gundar sprinkle! Others of your crew are there here? (*a falsehood dilute with truth confounds incredulity; one must take heed, and parse chaff and seed!*)

GRUNCH: All sleeping big, sir (groan). The Plutonian badbiters have eaten them up! I am the last of the loyalist faction (gasp) or I was, until you two came along. We survived earthyears of hellish inconvenience in utter blackness by tossing the bones of our big sleepers into the air and reassembling them! ...the backbone's connected to the hip-bone, the hip-bone's connected... but don't crank me up, sir! And then disassembling and retossing. This was our unwholesome pastime. Our old favorite, Ergbolt-the-Blackbox, doesn't work in here; we can't see well enough to write down positions and shots for postgame accounting. Too many of our big sleepers were cheaters. But forget them all! Now just me I'm! But no food for a week! Only tap water! BEWARE! (gurgle, gurgle).

EVA: Poor wretch! Don't they feed you? I should think they'd want a fat Petty-O. Here, have some fish 'n' chips. I stash'd 'em in my purse from lunch, you lucky Petty-O you.

GRUNCH: ....Yum, yum! BEWARE OF.. (chomp, gulp)

SNURL: My day is made, Grunch, by the noise of you enjoying your meal! But what did you state about the stones on which we stand? The "stones" which so abound are human bones! *(Every lining of silver is by a cloud enveloped.)*

CAPTIONS: Out of the blackness emerges a clutch of pecking badbiters, their eyes blazing filthy fire, and smelly stench penetrates the gloom. Eva Snarcesor screams and out she passes, as is the wont of woman. Grunch, accustomed to the vicissitudes of Plutonian existence, remains nonplused. Even so, a badbiter pecks off his leg. Only Lt. Snurl, true to the blue, seizes from the floor a femur and flails at the slavering badbiters, wreaking for them bad news. But to what avail? His foot slips in the same gore he has wrought, and he blacks out, ringing the curtain on Act Two, down.

Act III. Outside the cave, an hour later. The stars are blinking merrily.

SNURL: Cap'n Jick! O deceiving orbs, into my pate a corpse you do project! And bandaging the badbitten stump of Petty-O Grunch, moreover! What can my migrained mind believe? *(Yet what thy senses sense cannot mere nonsense be.)*

JICK: Yes, it's me, lad. I arrived in the nick of time, eh? Jick in the nick, ha ha. I and my trusty Excalizapp zapped ope the front door and blew the badbiters out the back. And here we are, basking in starlight.

SNURL: But how escaped you the crash? About we looked and peered, and couldn't spot your hairy hide!

JICK: There was no crash, Atom. I cannot but smile as I speak. We are the victims of an amusing hoax. We were tricked into thinking that we crashed. A big plastic-attractor machine was used to pull our spaceships from their path, the ships were captured, and then sold to the Astrogoths, who will soon have enough of them to invade earth and supplant Western Civilization with Astro Asceticism. Can you live with that?

SNURL: Never! The Tree of Liberty will be fertilized with the Blood of Ascetics! But back to the topic, Cap'n: the smoke, the ka-boom!, and the flames, billowing, billowing!

JICK: Dry ice, Dimension Sound, and mirrors, my lad. After the attractor diverts the ship from its course, a clever remote control takes over and guides the ship to a soft landing. Then, happy gas renders the crew inert, and ship and all are transported to an abandoned Plutonian theme park, where, when the crew awakes, vapor, reverb hi-fi, and multiple reflection complete the transaction. The bamboozled lads are allowed enough time to wire back home "S.O.S., Mayday, we crash!" and suddenly the communication is cut, adding to authenticity, and diddling the dupes at the VIDI. *Tutto nel mondo è burla.*

SNURL: Hilariously diabolical! And yet you made of them fools! How evaded you their nefariousness, and Eva and I, not so? *(The crew should not inherit, o Cap'n my Cap'n, thy sinking ship).*

JICK: There's a reason why I'm a cap'n and you're a
          lieutenant, Atom. A little bird told me, " Bail out, Jick."
          But you can't complain. Are you better off now than
          you were ten minutes ago? "Thank you, Cap'n Jick." By
          the way, we'd best get out of here.

SNURL: OK, bluejay, but Eva's where? With rage and anxiety
          am I beset! Off my shoulder git your motherless mitt, o
          Cap'n my Cap'n!

JICK: The last surviving badbiter seized Eva Snarcesor and
          carried her away to an unknown fate. I wanted to tell
          you, but I just didn't have the heart. By the way, you
          emote too much; you needn't exclaim everything. But
          now that the cat is unbagged, they went that way.

SNURL: Well, now that I know, Joe, let's go! Get up, Grunch, a
          maid to rescue before brunch have I got! Emotive or
          not!

Act IV. Down the road a piece.

CAPTIONS: They wend a painful way on the Plutonian
          plain. Following at a respectful distance behind
          Lt. Snurl and Cap'n Jick, Petty Officer Grunch
          is gamely hobbling along, aided by a makeshift
          crutch he has fashioned from somebody's ulna
          back at the boneyard. Several times they hear
          him slip and fall on the cruel icerocks of Pluto,
          but they know he is a fiercely proud old
          noncom, and any offer of assistance would
          likely just be another humiliation. So they
          pretend they don't hear him, and impatiently

wait for him to struggle to his foot. This time it was taking longer than usual. Jick points up at the sky.

JICK: From the icerocks, the lights begin to twinkle. Note the muddy gray spot, there, up in the air, Snurl. It is our earth, alas, so out of reach. Just think. If we could but pierce the murky atmosphere, we would be observing years in the future. You would be looking at your great-grandson looking at you through his gigascope, even though he's not yet conceived.

SNURL: But how can that, wise Cap'n, be? The reverse methought me: my great-granddad I'd see, through an old kiloscope peering he!

JICK: Your cosmological education terminated at Okefenokee U., eh, Atom? Mired in TV's Evening News, are you, with Dr. Deceit and Knightly Arrogance updating your database? How did you spend your domenical contemplations? "Hail Mary, let me know when this is over, zzzzzzzz," I'll wager. While I, on the other hand, introspected and solved great cosmic riddles. What was Tell telling us? The Law of the Apple, that's what. When the arrow pierces the apple on your head, as you look at the archer, he's already shot the arrow some time ago. But as the archer looks at you, he sees the consequence, the future. If the today is but an inevitable consequence of the past, the future is an inevitable consequence of the today. Its projection, along a relentless continuum. Translate this to rocketships and planets, jillions of miles, countless tickings of time, and the point is obvious. On one end, the past and on the other the future. A reaction equal and opposite. Escher's thousandword Leapin' Lizard Hypothesis extended this notion, and hooked yesterday and tomorrow together as the chain of lizards march round and round, in and out of the Artist's sketchpad. When it occurs to a lizard to raise his head, he'll see the future. If he turns around, he'll see the past. With a little googoloscope help, in either direction he'd see the Big Bang, which is the end of the cycle, and of course the beginning; the *Go* square, get it? We're contained by the *circularity* of time, lieutenant. *Selah.*

SNURL: What th'?! Have you jangled all your marbles? *Hel-lo,* Cap'n Jick! Your golden four-of-a-kind does beat my golden pair, but there's zip in the pot. Hark! Awaken! Old Grunch is back on his foot, and here we are, stuck on Pluto, in the old dingdong today. Focus, focus! As to those vicious badbiters, what? Dentate alar denizens! Why do they like chickens look, but like piranhas peck? And why do not they us pursue?

JICK: You must be ecstatic to be a lt., Snurl. Because we are so clever, cap'ns do have to think harder than you do. All these gold bars on my sleeve are just clutter, right? End of lecture, Lieutenant. Now, addressing your concerns, the egglayers brought along by crews were here simply Plutonized, and turned were the tables. Another case of Nature gone mad. In Pluto's netherworld, to relieve tedium, the buggers go on occasional wilding sprees and strip flesh off bones, when available. Except for the heads; they've been conditioned to set the heads aside for Mr. Vici. The boneyard back yonder is what remains of our hapless big sleepers, by the badbiters flayed and decapitated. They never venture above the surface because their tailfeathers freeze. But hey-de-ho, what before our very eyes is this?

SNURL:　　Mr. who, say you? Gadzooks! Here have we what? How says this banner on the door in this rock that before us looms?

JICK:　　"Mr. Vici welcomes all Bugboggers to peaceful Pluto! Please ring dingdong bell for joyous parade and happy ceremonies!"

SNURL:　　I sneer and scoff at Plutonian dissembling! But that reminds me, Grunch. Back yonder, of what were you bewaring us? Interrupted you were; the communication incomplete! *(The misfinished, to uninterpretation oft leads)*

GRUNCH:　　Cap'n Gundar! Beware of Cap'n Gundar! I forgot about Cap'n Gundar in all the excitement.

JICK:　　Yes, that filthy farrow is aligned with the Plutonian miscreants.

SNURL:　　About him, tell me! It was Gundar who unto the Plutonized poultry did us deliver! Inwardly do I retch at the thought of Eva at the mercy of a smelly badbiter! Say, who are the Bugboggers? And Mr. Vici, he is who? The bell do ignore, and with a quick zapp, ope the door! *(Occasion, men's mettle doth heckle!)*

JICK:　　Don't worry about Eva Snarcesor. The badbiters won't hurt her. I overheard them comment that they were to take her in one piece to Mr. Vici. I'll tell you about him presently. At one time, a thing, curious Snurl.

"Bugbog" is a snide Plutonian gibe at "planet earth." But step aside, as I zapp the bolted gate... Now, with shut mouths, do wend... Behold, the minions of Mr. Vici, the mortal instruments.

CAPTIONS: The frazzled travelers have rounded a corner into an unexpected throne room, with numerous weird figures scurrying about, the like of which are well beyond the Midwest imaginings of Lt. Snurl. He silently gasps, barely stifling an astonished gape. What he sees are oversized ears, noses, eyes, and mouths, all mounted on spidery legs. Some sport chipmunkish forepaws. On the throne is their group leader, King Mouth. Beside him are seated Prince Eye and Princess Ear.

JICK: I see you are wondering how these things function together, Atom. What coordinates these unappended appendages is a fantastically complex seat of intelligence that thinks collectively and transmits data to and from these modular members, his mortal instruments. The complex seat is the troublous genius known as Mr. Vici.

SNURL: Ahead of Lt. me, Cap'n Jick, you're always a leap and a half! Pray tell, *maestro*, in the entrails of this forsaken planet, whence the light and heat?

JICK: Just Plutonian radiation, Lt. you. It provides energy and eleven optional vitamins. But hark and look. The turncoat Gundar enters and approaches the throne.

KING: Here is your reward, Cap'n Gundar; you have served us

well. Is is my regal pleasure to present you with this official Slap-on-the-Back Letter.

GUNDAR: Big deal, you guys, big deal! I publicly snarl and burn silly backslap letter with cigarette lighter. Are you reneging on regal promise to turn over hotclucker Snarcesor ?

KING: I mete and dole unequal laws unto a savage race! Just kidding, a plutojoke, plutoho ho ho. Bring in *la Bugbogette!*

CAPTIONS: As Eva Snarcesor is brought forward, Snurl leaps to his feet, seizes Grunch's makeshift crutch, and batters his way through ears and noses. Jick is closely behind, zappadapping the scuttling creatures, and Grunch does what he can with his bare hands and teeth. But Jick's gun runs out of zapp, Grunch's teeth are rotten, and Snurl's borrowed crutch is worn to a stump. There are too many mortal instruments for our trio to trump. The hapless Eva Snarcesor grimaces as Gundar laughs triumphantly. The feisty earthtroopers are surrounded, bound, and carried away to horrors of a gross nature.

Act V. A sunken chamber, with menacing stalactites hanging about. In the center of the chamber yawns an abyss. Cap'n Gundar and a few mortal instruments are lording it over the immobilized quartet.

SNURL: Within this murky pit, behold the moving gray mass!

Can this be – it must be – the outlandish Mr. Vici!
(Howe'er grim the circumstance, the wonders of the firmament e'er amaze.)

JICK: You are a snailishly persistant pupil, Atom. You may indeed some day make the Big Four Club. But you've got to learn to talk like we do, and not contradict us.

GUNDAR: Mr. Vici is hungry, boys, and you are going to feed him! Just guys, Li'l Eva.

EVA: Think agin, Pinkeye. Somethin' will occur to Lt. Snurl to foil you!

GUNDAR: Enough palaver. Prepare for feast of brain!

JICK: Just what do you intend to do with this ridiculous machine with a lever, gauges, flashing lights and a hole at the top and at the bottom, you depraved idiot?

GUNDAR: You'll never know, Cap'n Jick!

CAPTIONS: Gundar unsheathes the sword at his side and neatly decollates Cap'n Jick. He throws the startled head into the top hole and pulls the lever. A crunch and a plop later, a glass jar emerges from the bottom hole, with gray matter that is clearly the brain of the ex-Cap'n. Against Gundar's triumphant snort play Eva Snarcesor's sobs and Snurl's crepitations. As Gundar tosses the gray blob into the mass below, Grunch attempts to make the best of a bad situation.

GRUNCH: Alas, poor Jick! Well, anyway, that's food for thought, eh kids? Hey, don't push me, Cap'n Gundar! I've only got one leg, I'll topple!

EVA: Snurl! Grasp the sword of Gundar! Grunch has fallen on an' squooshed the only eye sent by the mortal instrumen's! Note how they run about and bump inta each other; the blighters are blin' as batnicks!

SNURL: Try on this kick in the gutnick, Gundar, you space-age Benedict! This time, clown, for the long count you're down! And for your snicker-snee, *beaucoup merci*; this foil will us from our fetters free! For the exit, dear Eva, run; chattel no more art thou! Lo! Sliced are thy shackles! I follow, ooooooops!

EVA: Snurl, as before, you have slipped on a gory floor, and what's more, now you have fallen inta th' abyss o' Mr. Vici's mindmass! *Hasta la vista, mon chéri*; here, I'm outa !

Act VI. In the Abyss. A cosmogonic dialogue.

SNURL: A sinner I'm! On my soul, Milord, mercy have! But OUCH !! Why have I stopped hurtling? Egad, detained am I by a stalagmite from the side of the pit sidewinding, piercing my bum! O serendipity! *No fat lady, no final curtain, for the fortuitous.*

MR. VICI: You have penetrated into my physical consciousness, Lt. Snurl. Those that do are merged into me. It is only a question of time before I absorb you, your spirit, your essence, your mind into mine. Make it easy for you and me both, and join me voluntarily. It will not take long for mortal instrument replacement eyes to arrive and direct the casting of bones at you until you tumble. Save yourself the embarrassment and just slip off.

SNURL: What th'!! My marbles I have mislaid! Voices I hear bypassing my ear!

MR. VICI: Your mind functions properly. We're just a couple of telepathizers, you and I. Now that I, Mr. Vici, have conquered you, Lt. Snurl, I don't mind telling you that I am relishing the experience. I seldom have occasion to communicate *tête-a-tête* with an independent mind. I know many, many things that you could never dream of; you know very little that I do not. And most of the things that you know, you don't know at all. Nevertheless, I admit I do enjoy this conversation. It is more stimulating than just autothinking off-the-wall thoughts.

SNURL: It I get! An analogy, yet: tiresome it must be, with only one piece on the board, playing Monopoly by yourself!

MR. VICI: Alone I do play my games, but with more than one piece on the board; however, you are amusing, and not entirely off the map. Do you not wonder, Lt. Snurl, what game I am really playing? Can it be the same game that you yourself are playing not knowing that you are playing a game? But what would you know of epistemological cosmology?

SNURL: I be not as unlettered as you think I be, Mr. Bigfat Vici! At the U. of Okefenokee I did well in Cosmological Epistemology! Without it, no space cadet louie goes aloft! At your pleasure on Cartesian semantics, quiz me! *(A bigfat brainpan, the modest wimple of wisdom warms not.)*

MR. VICI: Well then, as we are compeers, allow me to level with you. I was originally a Plutonian rock, conscious only of consciousness. A wandering *tabula ex machina* came bouncing by and smashed into my rocky awareness. Like a cometic camera, these *tabulae* lack awareness but sport mobility and perception. Just what I needed! I suddenly found knowledge. Now I had a bank of data to measure and compare; I could now, in a word, think. Although entrapped and immobile, I passed many Plutonian moons exploring this really useful ability.

SNURL: Holy Jehoshaphat, what an anecdote! But how claustrophobically uncomfortable! Tantamount to burial! You could not move! You could not see! Nor feel! Even smell was denied you! How could you your sanity maintain under such restriction?

MR. VICI: Why, mind games, me lad. You take what you have, break it down, reconstruct, and create your own universe. Consider: I had never known any of those sensory experiences, and hence could feel no anguish at their absence. I constructed a Plutonian language, and from it spun myriad tongues. It pleased me to interpret the same data using descriptors encased in differing language schemes. Although the landscape of my mind remained the same, describing it in differing tongues made it appear changefully fresh. And some of the effects resulting were so much more pleasing to me than others.

SNURL: A blessing, the Babel Tower! A boon, the confounded language! But of course! *Mit diesem Zeichen bann' ich deinen Zauber: wie die Wunde er schliesse, die mit ihm du schlugest, in Trauer und Trümmer stürze die trügende Pracht!* would sound silly in Anglojabber.

MR. VICI: *Der witsigste bist du unter den Weisen!* But, my young wit, I was not through with wordplay: I developed a palindromic system that amuses me to this day. As in RE: VENUS; TEN-ALP PLANET, SUN EVER! Let me amuse you with an improv demonstration: give me a random word.

SNURL: Humor thee shall I! We too are veteran palindromers! Ever since "MADAM I'M ADAM," with facility we earthlings bounce 'em out! Here's a sly one: MARY'S PIG SAM DID NOT RUB BURTON. DID MA'S

GIPSY RAM? *Voilà!* Your challenge I accept! For Olympian you, here's a suggestive word for starters: "ZEUS." *(The best defense is oft a brown nose.)*

MR. VICI: Methinks you do know the game. *En garde,* Mr. Smartaleck, try and top this: ZEUS, REVILED, SET A RIP-KNIFE. NO RED WOP, DELBERT WAS RAW. GODDAMN MAD DOG! WARSAW TREBLED (POWDER ONE FINK). PIRATES DELIVER SUEZ. Pretty nifty, eh? And here's a slangy Anglojabber lead-in for you, Bugbog wordsmith: "LOOKY."

SNURL: Why yes, wordsmith if you will, extempore. *Audite* with your mind's ear and *videte* with your brain's eye: LOOKY AT STINKER PATTON'S NOTE: NO SIAM GEMS, MARGE, NO DETOXIFIED SUPOSITORY PEELS. OHO! SNIDE WOLF-MURDERS A HYANNIS SIN? NAY! HAS RED RUM FLOWED IN SOHO? SLEEPY ROT IS OPUS DEI. FIX, O TED! (ONE GRAM SMEGMA IS ONE TON SNOT.) TAP, RE-KNIT, STAY KOOL.

MR. VICI: Enough of your tasteless *legerdeparole,* earthling. Suppository is misspelled, "kool" is entirely unacceptable, and your stretched-out palindrome is obfuscatingly metaphorical. They'll be awarding you a Nobel. But we do digress so. I think my point is well made. List to my arduous journey of realization: I ideated an internal TV with ever-changing programming for passive amusement. Allow me to plug in you to channel 2.

SNURL: Wowie! A bunch of funny blinking spangles I do perceive! And into other bizarre glitter they gradually morph! What is it? A Kleinbottle kaleidoscope, peering back at synapseflash in my brain? This is no TV set. Impressed am I not, unplug me do.

MR. VICI: So what pseudorandom events tickle *your* fandango? Shake up your stereotypes and basic situations and let them aimlessly bump into each other for an eon or two. That's Bugbog TV. Allow me to venture a comment as to the special problems involved in providing entertainment over eternity: you will find it more efficient to jiggle the sensor rather than fiddle with the sensed. But eventually I did tire of my TV. The same patterns appeared to be recycling. I was unable to generate a really random sequence. It dawned on me that I needed to extend my reach to activity not under my direct control, but which could provide me with real-time feedback involving external occurrences. I longed to be surprised by something I had not already imagined. Thus I willed the creation of my mortal instruments, controlled by my telepathic powers, to aid me in mobility and observation. They were able to transmit to me images in apparent disarray, and provide me with random number tables for my mental games! They also enabled me to capture most of the available intelligent life forms my *tabula* had revealed to be on

Pluto. I then enhanced my pool of thought by the same osmotic process that permitted me to absorb the *tabula* itself. All that I have met, is of me a part.

SNURL: Impressive! But the point is what? Just a bigger and smarter cephalic index you want to be? All cerebrum and no psyche? No six-packs and no wenching? *(The pleasures of life are derived though visceral distraction, not through the rigors of cerebration.)*

MR. VICI: Yes, scrofulous pastimes do provide diversion. They do not instruct. Alternatively, the cycle of enlightenment goes from the excitement of wanting to know, and learning until everything is known, and then absolute boredom, and wanting not to know, yearning for the excitement of learning all over again with a clean slate. And then doing it. Reality is not changed, only the perception of it.

SNURL: It I do get, gov'nuh! The googolopiece jigsaw resolved, in the air you toss her, to again begin! *(The sun rises to view nothing new, and ice is still only O & H2!)*

MR. VICI: You have glimpsed a cosmic notion with an unmerged mind: all matter's elements are just rearrangements of the same old pieces from the same old Tinkertoy can. Join me; we will ultimately advance to *Go* and reach the apex of knowledge. I have absorbed the minds of countless Plutonians and all

Bugbog crews. Eva Snarcesor and Grunch cannot escape me. When the Astrogoths conquer Bugbog, every Bugbog mind will be merged into mine. The Astrogoths will be next.

SNURL: *(Blast me turbos, Vici is the thwarter of VENI and VIDI! And he is using the Astrogoths his schemes to further, but at his convenience these unsuspecting ascetics he will also betray! Well, at least the space engineers back home can with relief sigh. Off the hook is their dozing and bumbling! Snurl, to this looneytoon speak softly.)* Say, where'd you come up with the cool moniker, "Vici"?

MR. VICI: Well, let me tell you, little Bugbogger. 'Way back in prehistory, they called me the Plutonian Rock, or just "PR." That gave me a notion. A little PR could light the fuse! So I dubbed myself Mr. *Victorious Interplanetary Capturer of Images;* in acronymic parlance, "Mr. VICI." My career took off. But you do prejudge me. My trajectory has been righteously paved with good intent. I seek truth and cosmic oneness. My unified theory of the immutability of time will save the universe much wearisome twiddling. Say, please concentrate better lieutenant, your thought transmission is fuzzing up.

SNURL: *(With care this mindfield must I trod and selectively my thoughts transmit)* With due respect, dogooder Vici, it's the *deeds* that earn the Ribbons; the *good intentions,* not even Honorable Mentions. Methinks much misinformation you may have sucked up, together with the good stuff! Versed you are in the Law of the Apple? *Processed data and knowledge are cousins, but much removed.*

MR. VICI: You just don't get it, do you, lieutenant? You presume to test me? The "Law" you refer to was just a trick of Cap'n Jick, as you suspected. I absorb the thoughts of all minds, and they are all cross-referenced. There is a reconciliation. The Law of the Apple is fraught with semantic sleight; Cap'n Jick was testing your deference to authority. He was probing your mettle for battlefield promotion, and you flunked the test.

SNURL: Jick yet another antihero clayfoot! How abashed can I get? Behold a somewhat convinced Snurl! Tell me, o supreme eclectic dBase so magnificently indexed, does each absorbed mind individually retain its self-awareness? Are Jick's ears a-burning?

MR. VICI: Pish, lieutenant. Even if not, who cares? I am aware of all that Jick was aware of. For me, absorbing Jick was just another learning experience, like reading a book. His entire awareness is now merged with mine own. You might say he just had a BIG BIG learning experience. Kind of like instant growing up. So in a sense, in talking to me you are addressing a new and improved Jick.

SNURL: In a sense, Jick's old essence is the Home He Can't Go Again! *(Sentimental wax I. Back to pragmatic I wane!)* Bye-bye, Cap'n Jick; howdy-do Mr.Vici, intellect beyond mortal comprehension compounded! Ergo, on with the show! Hounded am I by an innocent curiosity that wants to know! For sex, in what activity do you engage? Or have you renounced pleasure, as they say, of the flesh, in relentless quest for universal influence?

MR. VICI: I renounce a big zip, Lieutenant. All avenues must be explored in order to make a map. Your curiosity is legitimate; at truth's bashes, impertinence is ever a crasher of gates. I require no mortal instruments to stimulate my earth-absorbed somatosenses, I just push, as it were, a mental button. All pleasure and all pain are buttons in the brain. My surrogate eyes and ears gather cosmic information; the buttons assist me in interpreting the iota that has to do with the Bugbog stuff. The art of Michelangelo, Maya Angelou & Marilyn Monroe would be a mystery to me without a little button pushing.

SNURL: Stuff, maestro? Of eternal and universal verities these are embodiments! In time encapsulated! Into space capsules launched to woo and confound extraterrestrial sensibilities! Pentameters, curves, hues, and modulations of OSCAR stature breaking through the Orion Belt barrier, E.T. and his ilk to duly astonish! *Beethoven on Betelgeuse will big business be.*

MR. VICI: Babbittbabble, lieutenant. Your Paganinis

and Picassos are just Dadaist jerks here on Pluto. The buttons they push are found only in the heads of Bugboggers like yourself. They were admired for what they did where they did it, but it's like writing the constitution of the state of Tabasco on a pinpoint. It's only a bestseller in the *Lagunilla*. Here on Pluto we had our own button-pushers, but their plutosublime efforts would look like blipstatic to you. You see, while scientists search without, artists look within; scientists synthesize, constructing unity and unvarnished truth for the greater community, while artists analyze, disassembling into diversity and varnished diversion for the parochial crowd. Mind you, I'm not knocking the tunespinners and talesmiths. The down-cycle is just as important as the up-cycle in the job of combating cosmic ennui. You have to unlearn in an orderly fashion if you intend to get to the bottom with any thought of a return ticket, and that voyage itself indeed may be half the fun. I am ready to reassemble the puzzle. The mountain's there for me to go up; getting back to the top is at least the other fun half. And more edifying.

SNURL: What! The down-cycle is Shakespeare, Saint-Saens, and a night on the town? Wait! It I do get it I do! Jaded and banged-up you'd get slaloming down forever! And *Principia Matematica* on your way back on the T-bar you can read! You're a regular can-do solipsistic Sisyphus! All over again to orgy, a nap you've got to take, a hearty breakfast eat, and a glance or two take at the Daily Prate!

MR. VICI: I think you're getting somewhere, lieutenant. Except there's no T-bar; it's pretty much a do-it-yourself exercise. Each little step a victory as you move upward, learning, anticipating--- to finally achieve the view from the top. I'll make you a once-in-your-lousy-life offer: If you don't care to join me here, I can instruct you as to setting up another up-cycle brain center on Bugbog. We have a training academy on Pluto for that purpose. We have already helped to establish centers on Titania, Ariel, Nereid, and Charon. Can we sign you up for the next semester? You will be the first Bugbogger so honored.

SNURL: O great compendium of cosmic cerebration! Unwarranted accolade you do confer on this humble officer junior! But forgive a sincere skeptic's stance! Inform me, in their endeavors have your alumni prospered and palpably advanced your project?

MR. VICI: All have progressed well, except for Charon. I can only teach; I cannot control. The brain center there is dedicated to down-cycle button-pushing, with their mortal instruments programmed for maintenance and wake-up operations. This bodes bad tidings. An amplified and unstoppable thrill is the definition of pain.

SNURL: But reflect, maestro, the Charonese will bottom with
             such impact that they will to the summit rebound with
             breathless acceleration! Perhaps just a question of
             technique? Consider their commendable forethought in
             preprogramming the instruments! *(High-jinks unhinged
             do require a designated driver.)*

MR. VICI: Your observation is cleverly worded, but
             hardly applicable. Personally. I think they're
             just goofing off. In any event, their agenda
             is not my own. And is there any guarantee
             that the mortal instruments would still be
             around at Armageddon? Let me pose a
             quodlibet: would you willingly fall asleep
             knowing as you relinquish consciousness
             that your dreams could be interminable,
             that they might take unanticipated and
             disagreeable turns, and that you might
             never return to reality, as unpleasant or as
             boring as it might have been?

SNURL: A false dilemma up do you conjure, wise Abu Ben
             Guru, but if your palaver I properly penetrate, about
             that let me reply: release of consciousness, of course,
             but unconditionally, no, never! Even so, back to a
             boring reality, a big rush neither! In the beginning, if
             everything was known, that was the problem. Power
             corrupts, which after all might be fun! But absolute
             power must be boring. Reverse course, decentralize!
             Your awareness, break up into teensy pieces; apportion
             them to your mortal instruments; implant seeds of
             reversion, like Hansel's pebbles, and throughout the

universe scatter them! Beget and be reborn, and the same old stuff learn to view anew! The Charonese have got it right! With the flow, go, go go! Best scenario: release consciousness, regain same eventually and irrevocably, but of no essence is time, zip, zero, *nada*; it's eternity we're dealing with! *(Marry, merely to those who sell clocks, of import is time.)*

MR. VICI: You fool, your own leg you pull. As you spiral and sputter down, down, down, your task of reconstructing original consciousness becomes infinitely more complex. Pardon my passion, but at some point the stone must be rolled up again. Eternity schmernity, the chips are down and splintering.

SNURL: Passion schmashin, o overwise collage of hodgepodge! The jigsaw you would reassemble is not merely at any point in time a big job, but the pieces themselves are incomplete, eternally propagating and evolving, impossibilitating your backtogethering them ever! Let entropy chart her course! The scientific knowledge you accrue attends to comfort, curiosity, longevity, and addiction to velocity. However, not only can the final piece of your galactic jigsaw never be in place, what makes you think that any pieces would fit together at all? The summit you will have reached is a unidimension jackspeck in an infidimension mansion! Like, could the Black Box Beta squad, in Spaceland, ever celebrate a meeting of minds with the crew of *Sink the Battleship*, in Flatland? Assuming you arrive at a conclusion regarding everything that you can imagine, about what you can't imagine, what? Is not the artist who his own feelings explores, the more likely to sense the unattunable? Within our galactic view the cosmos resides not, but in our DNA rather! *(In Gut We Trust.)*

MR. VICI: Are you suggesting that my life work is nothing much? My theories so far leave you unimpressed? Nothin' yet, you ain't heard! I've a jillion more of 'em! Ye have heard from old Jick that time is circular. Pfaagh! I say unto you that time is *immutable.* Time doesn't exist at all, it's just a tricky way of measuring any one of the dimensions you can see. Remember Old Johnny "Clockjock" Harrison? His marine chronometer measured nautical miles in terms of lapsed hours, exposing "time" as just distance wrapped around a "clock," just as a fish line is wrapped around a reel. Everything that was, is, and will be, is everever present, but you only observe it piece by piece, and in one direction, as out it reels. Like a movie. It's all there, spread out on a manyfoot reel, but you see it frame by frame, and create the illusion of time. Recall Dobson's Paradox: "Time stays, *we* go." Stick with me, kid, and I'll give you a proof you can't refute. In the meantime, reconciling and fitting together my myriad and proprietary apocalyptics is a big jigsaw job.

SNURL: Your impressive theories have indeed provoked in me an AHA! moment or two. Hear ye me, Mr. Vici! On board the *Excelsior,* pondering the isosceles poser, to me it occurred that the proof was *reversible;* the conclusion, back to the givens, can lead! I came to realize that many things, like chemical equations, were obviously reversible. What was gradually to me revealed was that *all* things, theoretically reversible are! Eternal nights spent on the *Excelsior*, on autopilot, nothing to do but endless yo-yo tournaments and viewing of ancient films, for new experience we finally played the movies backward. Yea, those manyfoot reels are just as convincing when backward played! At this very moment insightful inspiration doth yo-me-yo from top to toe! Not the circularity, nor immutability, but the *reversibility* of time! When we reach the end of the cosmic reel, in reverse it will automatically play to return to the opening credits! It is thus predestined. The graves open and age regresses to youth, which crawls back into the womb, and on and on, and the world returns to Genesis, Chap. I, Verse 1! And, ultimately, to the unwritten prologue. It's not that *I Yam* isn't; He's selfsmithereened, and the premises abandoned! There's no one in charge Upstairs because *I Yam* is Himself the googolopiece puzzle! You and I and all our cosmos aren't even one pixel on a piece of that whopperongous jigsaw. Rolling back up the stone, for you a preposterous endeavor. Reassembling the Big Picture, all that forget. It's preset to happen anyhow, but not by you. *I-Yam-What-I-Yam* to Primal Consciousness will restored be! But you know what? It's late. SO I DARE, GALLAGER, ADIOS! *(For the dramatic denouement all conversations of grand moment intuit the moment.)*

MR. VICI: When you can't arguefy 'em, decapitate 'em and suck 'em up! GUARDS!

CAPTIONS: Lt. Snurl does not tarry to banter further with this engaging but murderous conversationalist. He has observed a *vineus tarzanus ex machina* close at hand, leading to the orifice above. He clambers up the vine and leaps out of the pit just as the army of mortal instruments summoned by Mr. Vici turn the corner. Wounded backside notwithstanding, his earthlegs outdistance the spindlelegs appendages, and he is soon marathoning alone on the vast Plutonian plain. He looks upward, saluting his imagined grandfather, or grandson -- or could it be he himself? -- watching out yonder. Suddenly, inexplicably, he finds himself before the spaceship *Excelsior*. A hatch opens, a drawbridge lowers, and Lt. Snurl enters his old rocket home.

Act 7. The *Excelsior* Reunion.

SNURL: Thou, Eva Snarcesor! Mine eyes deceive my bumblebrain! Why didst not thou escape when thou couldst? My heart brimmeth over! For me, all this time thou hast waited!

EVA: Alas, an embarrassed lass am I, Cap'n Snurl. Honest Indiana, I wrote off you as a goneroo. With her life, a girlie's gotta get goin'. I'm still here because I couldn' get this clunker spacecraf' t' start up! Nayther could th' bloomin' Astrogoths, I reckon, w'ich is why *Excelsior* was still here. But first let me apply this healin' Astyptodyne© t' that bloody bum, ol' chum!

SNURL: Indeed, thou'rt a Nightingale in need! But what's with the cap'n stuff? Thou knowest I am a lowly lieut. Thou'rt rubbing it in, *mamacita* masseuse. *(Never so low art thou that a sarcastic slap can't bop thee below bottom.)*

EVA: You darlin' fool, Atom Snurl, look at this secret directive, signed by Commissioner O'Nuker herself. I'm a Spacefleet Adm'ral, t' take charge in event o' any male bumblin'! On board is P-Off'cer Grunch, but he's got a "Latrine Police" MOS, an' other than as an Ergbolt-the-Blackbox easy mark, he's nexta useless. He's polishin' th' porcelain in th' lassies' loo richt noo. My first official act is t' promote you t' cap'n; and my secon' is t' order you to get this ship outa this Plutonian 'musement park and onta th' spaceroad again!

SNURL: Wowie! Unceasing wonder! Ambition realized! This Cap'n salutes thee, Admiral mine. But 'tis thy homespun palaver ever uttering that from the mooing herd so sets thee apart, heifer-o'-ma-heart! Didst remember the clutch to push down whilst the ignition keying? All late model space vehicles this safety feature do boast. Ye dainty lassies find this tough laddie technology stuff so plaguy.

EVA: O fam'ly values o' langsyne! You men are so mechan'cal! Ver'ly, I do need thee, me virile Atom Snurl. That detail indeed me maiden's min' did slip! The good news is that those would-be invadin' Astrogoth sissies didn' think of it ayther. Earth is safe! Now, off t' Arcturus, the universe t' pop'late! Beyon' th' sunset t' sail!

SNURL: With cap'nly respect, thy order I countermand, o most admirable Admiral soon-to-be Snurl *née* Snarcesor! But we gotta point out to Commissioner O'Nuker the peril Vici poses, inamorata! Later or sooner the Astrogoths will about the clutch trick, from Vici ascertain. O'Nuker must us debrief and Vici's galactic nonsense stop! Back to earth we go, our navels to observe. Better a bug in thy bog than a badbiter in thy bum! I must a tree, plant; a son, raise; and a book, write! Let us warm, Eva mine, to the universe within. *(Others may strive and seek and never yield, but they will not find what they are not built to perceive.)*

CAPTIONS: Admiral Snarcesor cannot but submit to this seductive mutiny. She steps on the clutch, pertly winks at Cap'n Snurl, turns on the ignition, and aims earthward. After many harrowing episodes, our heroes are hurtling home to the still dwellable, but drying-up, earth, air, and oceans of the Bugbog Planet.

Red Is July

The following is an excerpt from the foreward to the textbook *See Spot Smell! See Spot Smell Jane's Fuzzy Armpit!* -- an *American Reader for Curious Modern Pubescents,* by Asar Alubat, Chair, Child Manipulation Studies, Okefenokee U.

Welcome to your first sashay into the literary thicket of American Lit., all you unbaptized little cerebra! Barney and Big Bird were just cynical old perverts in freaky frippery, right? And Howdy Doody is dead! Gone are the sunny meadows of Hansel, Gretel, and Red Riding Hood.

Gird yourselves, kids, for some REAL dragons and some itchy situations! Nat Hawthorne is here, and creepy Eddie Poe, and -- look out! "Pops" Hemingway and Shirl-the-Girl Jackson! No friendly, shady oaks in sight; just hard-drinkin', tell-it-like-it-is, rappin' poison oaks. Prepare to have your sniffy little noses rubbed in shrubbery that you can relate to! These mighty he-men and she-women lived through it all to tell you the story. Keep your beady eyes open and you may spot some really cool she-men and he-women in the brush.

Some of these dudes have been dead for a century or so, but hey! what they wrote is more relevant today than it was when they wrote it. To guide you through this new relevancy, we have provided groovy hints and fun teeniebop quizzes. These also serve to make the life of your teach a little easier. After all, he's got problems of his own to relate to.

RED IS JULY

PLAYERS:

GROSVENOR, A DISGRUNTLED REDNECK
BERGSMA, A SELFLESS BESPECTACLED WIFE
JEREMY, A YOUTH MANIPULATED BY GROSVENOR

... AND BEHIND THE SCENES BUT PRESENT:

YOU! YES, YOU. SIT STRAIGHT AND PAY ATTENTION.
HOMEWORK IS DUE AT BEGINNING OF MRS. DEFARGE'S
CLASS TOMORROW.

(A conversation with *you*)

 Grosvenor muttered as he mopped his salty brow. Nothing had happened today. He had been sitting for an hour on the porch with a little bag of rock candy, hoping that Prissy Phillips might strut by en route to the A & P, but it was not to be. However, Jeremy would be arriving soon with some cold Kool-Aid, and that was a refreshing idea. It's called Kool-Aid for a reason. You pour it in your glass and it aids you to be kool. Kool is cooler than cool.

What did Grosvenor have in mind for Prissy Phillips? Something seems wrong with the title of this story. How would you fix it?

It was an unduly hot summer evening, and the subdued buzzerama of cicada was just beginning to grate on his ear. He ground his callousy football into the splintery porchfloor, wondering if he should go inside or stay put. The crunchy noise of hard callous against dry wood provided further irritation, so he made up his mind to abandon the porch and go on inside. Catching the handle of the screendoor with his cane, he pulled it open, and beheld an inert black spot self-resurrect and buzz through the open door. Then he got up and followed the buzzbug, the screen slamming behind him.

What were the cicada attempting to communicate to Grosvenor? How does the buzzbug set the mood for what is about to happen? What do you get if you mix a buzzbug with a diet colt?

Bergsma was just finishing up with the dinner dishes, and Grosvenor observed her labored breath and sweat-soaked blouse with a sense of power and control. She was a hard-working woman; he was proud of her, and he felt that their contractual relationship had been a good arrangement for both. She seldom contradicted him, and took the "love, honor, obey" clause seriously. In return, he had fed, clothed and sheltered her for most of her life.

What do you think Bergsma had prepared for dinner? Do you think Bergsma ever entertained a notion to slip something "special" into Grosvenor's gumbo? Could she learn a trick or two from Martha Stewart?

He noticed the domino set extended out about the card table from his last game with Bergsma. He studied the tree of tiles, attempting to recreate the game, in a futile attempt to determine a strategy to follow. Bergsma's honoring of her husband did not include intentionally allowing him to defeat her at dominoes. It was a tiny tit in return for a big tat, but it provided satisfaction. She didn't rub it in, though. She attributed her skill to good luck, and Grosvenor's ego allowed him to swallow that at face value. There is such a thing as the luck of the draw, and especially in dominoes, but you do have to be a pretty bad player to lose all the time. Of course, like in so many parlor games, the trick is to remember who doesn't play what when they would have if they'd had it, but that never occurred to Grosvenor, who seldom won at anything.

What would Grosvenor win if he beat Bergsma at dominoes? Wouldn't you rather watch "Who Wants To Be a Millionaire" than play dominoes?

Hearing footsteps, he looked up to see Jeremy coming up the walk, Kool-Aid in hand, and Grosvenor silently cursed. It was still light enough for him to make out the pale reddish color of the liquid in the glass pitcher, and he knew that it was strawberry. Raspberry red is a deeper color than strawberry red, and grape, of course, is not red at all. It could only be strawberry, and he knew that Jeremy knew that he did not like strawberry. The ice cubes jangled annoyingly as Jeremy came up the steps and entered the room. He neglected to pull the screen tightly to, and noticing the scowl on Grosvenor's face, he turned to pull the screen into place. Grosvenor was still scowling when Jeremy turned to him again, and as the ice clanked embarrassingly, Jeremy suddenly realized that he had *really* done it. He had brought the one flavor disfavored by Grosvenor. The raspberry jar of Kool-Aid and the strawberry jar of Kool-Aid looked the same in his dark pantry, and Jeremy had simply goofed. How to explain this to Grosvenor? It was not possible.

Why do you think Grosvenor did not like strawberry Kool-Aid? What flavor don't you like?

Jeremy glanced down at the dominoes on the table before him, and Grosvenor knew that he was about to attempt a diversionary gambit. Jeremy looked into the fuming man's squinty eyes and realized that Grosvenor was aware of his plan, and because he was actually afraid to disappoint him, charged ahead and blurted, "Figgerin' out a way to beat Bergsma, Gros?" Immediately he knew that he had made the mistake of poking at Achilles' heel. The attempted diversion compounded the crime.

Why is Jeremy so subservient to Grosvenor? Do you think Jeremy has a girl friend?

Grosvenor tried to think of a snappy putdown, but maybe it was the heat. He made no reply, and sullenly played with his dominoes. Jeremy looked down at the Kool-Aid in his hand, damned strawberry, damned red, brightly proclaiming his incompetence to the accompaniment of the icecube chorus. He sighed and went into the kitchen.

List five snappy retorts Homer Simpson would have come up with to skewer Jeremy, heat or no heat.

Bergsma was wiping off the stove with the dishrag. Jeremy smiled at her and proffered the colored liquid. She nodded, peering over her greasy spectacles, and in a surge of motherly compassion gushed, "Sure, go ahead,-- it's better than drinkin' plain old tap water, anyhow." As he slopped the liquid into a glass, he looked into Bergsma's spectacles and barely made out the image of Grosvenor standing behind him.

This is the first full-brush portrait we have of Bergsma, and yet we feel we have known her all her life. What greasy, motherly actress would you cast in her role? How is it subtly suggested that Jeremy might be Bergsma's secret "love-child"?

Bergsma did her best. "Come on, Gros, it's better than plain water. Jeremy was just tryin' to please you." She might as well have been talking in pigLatin. Grosvenor just stared at the unhappy chap who had just tried to please, but who was now ready to licketysplit. "Get out of here," he said quietly and ominously. "Get out of here, Jeremy."

How would you say "Jeremy was just trying to please you" in pig Latin? For extra credit, turn in your next U.S. History homework assignment in pig Latin.

Jeremy felt very cold and very, very persecuted and he blinked his eyes. He backed out of the kitchen, out of the living room, and scooted down the front walk. The screen door opened and the pitcher flew after him, shattering into wet fragments on the hot asphalt, and Jeremy ran like hell all the way home.

What does Jeremy learn from this visit? How can he pump up his self-esteem? What could Grosvenor do to live a more fulfilling life in the future? Rewrite the final paragraph to make it more appropriate for prime-time television.

Ans. to conundrum on p. 118: Either Buzz Liteyear, or a bugling.

SONGS

Verses
of
AntiSocial
Significance

The Croaking of a Fink

The day my mother called me goy
I wept into my cornflakes bowl.
Sticks and stones may break your bones
But words can sear your soul.

Sticks and stones and
words are inanimate

I broke her shiksa neck that night
And schlepped her to the drink.
Her days of pain and pang are past.
And me? I kvetch to a pricey shrink.

But words are an excuse for
antisocial animation

The Children Complain of Neglected Bathrooms

Pop went lookin' for a lover
but he chanced upon a whore
an' now that it's a habit
he keeps goin' back for more.
If our misguided parent
had imagination
instead of seekin' substitutes
he'd practice masturbation.
Th' drains are plugged, we're all alone,
an' dunno what to do.
For pop is in a bawdyhouse
an' mom is at the pub.
We wish they'd hurry home
because we feel a little blue.
There's flotsam in the toiletbowl
an' jetsam in the tub.

Fox Trotting in Tacoma

The shotwads of Nevernevermore
bump kneecaps on Saturday night.
(To wheezy strains they staunchly ape
  the rock of life
  under mottled pastel light
  that brings to surface sad and jaundiced souls)
Recognizing the strange and changing faces
synchronized with the syncopation of disconnect
they *Shuffle Off to Buffalo*
to the slosh of their dish of tea.

SWALLOWED UP IN VICTORY

Hostias

**Bring me brandy, cried the man,
so grimly gaunt, and failing fast.
Ply me well with *pulque*, pals
each gasping breath may be my last.**

In Paradisum

***FETCH ME FLESH, HE CRIED AGAIN,
GATHER ME GIRLIES GALORE,
DEATH'S ANGEL HOVERS NEAR ME,
HE BECKONS AT THE DOOR.***

Dies Irae

**GET GOSPELS, GODS, & HOLY GHOSTS,
HE SHRIEKED AS IF IN PAIN,
FOR I CAN FEEL THE CLAMMY CLAW
OF DEATH UPON MY BRAIN.**

Requiem Aeternam

WE BROUGHT HIM BOOZE
WE BROUGHT HIM SEX,
WE PROPPED HIM UP WITH BIBLES.
BEFORE HE DIED
WE CAUGHT THE GLINT
OF HEAVEN IN HIS EYEBALLS.

Off to the Fat Planet, by Jove

Let's tallyho for Callisto
my merry, startanned men; on the
Amalthean grass we'll cool our heels
and then begin again.
Let's pile up speed for Ganymede,
my hairyarmpit crew; at a
cornucopian urn await our turn
to quaff the devil's brew.
We'll goose some jovial maidens
And guzzle jovial gin; by the
morrow's dawn we'll all be gone
To space's depths again.
And if you meet those jovial guys
who think Jupiter's so nize, tell 'em
earth may not be the immensest,
but it's the densest.

2001 MADE SIMPLE

WITH PASSION ACHROMATIC
IN CELESTIAL ORGASM
  HE SPEWED THE SKIES
    WITH HIS GLISTENING GYZM

NESTLED IN THE MILKY WHITENESS OF A MILLION STARS
HIS SCHIZOID SPERM
  MOVE WITH SIDEREAL PATIENCE
    TOWARD A THRESHOLD OF EXISTENCE

THE NONSOLIPSIST OFFSPRING HAS YET
                    TO BE CONCEIVED

The Antidepressant Dealer

What this country needs
Said FDR in thirtythree,
Is warmed-over Social-ism
Fala and Moosejaw and me.
By nineteen hundred fortyone
He found his nostrums didn't stick.
To bring the unemployment down,
A Fight for Freedom does the trick.

The Artist Reconsidered

She stared at the reams of white.
Her keyboard stuttered while she diddled
until a notion leapt from head to fingers
and the notion morphed to pica pica pica
before her eyes! Her perspectives, her visions
took form. Fasterandfasterandfaster she wrote,
freely, undeliberately, synapses crackling.
"My notion I shall spam to the stars!"
she cockadoodledoo'd,
"The universe shall buzz with my notion!"
She stopped, did a monalisa,
ripped the pages to confetti,
cast them to the spirits of the air
and felt the pangs of genius unacclaimed.

Another Whole Year Older

Not that they don't rhyme
not that they don't scan
not that they aren't convenient
nor commodious
nor technicolored and sometimes even cute
But because they do
rhyme & scan & are too full of it
I mean convenience & commodity
& are too garish & gaudy & tawdry & cute
They don't sound like me an' you a-tall
& maybe I want to express
something other than a buck's worth of
happy birthday pardner

Mother's Day

putting one's lineage
on a pedestal
smacks of a hackneyed sort of
narcissistic backhanded
backslapping routine
it being a reasonably
scientific theory
that heredity and environment
determine the individual
not to on the appointed occasion
heap garlands
on the brows of those chiefly responsible
for one's pre- and post-
natal environment
to say nothing of all that heredity
is missing a chance to by association
prove one's self a pretty good
joe after all

Ding-Dong Daddy's Day

Consistent with the spangled notions of the American dream
Your neighborly friendlihood dealers have decreed
that a convenient Sunday in June be set aside as
     DING-DONG
     F*A*T*H*E*R'S D*A*Y
What's good for your father is
Gold for the Nat'l Ass'n of Merchants
Dear old dad certainly deserves a cut
In some of that heady adulation left over from last month's
     M*O*T*H*E*R'S D*A*Y
celebration
And besides how convenient to effect
Efficient conversion of May's banners and placards
 to those more appropriate for June and (Ho for the
 paterfamilia) dear old stud
Simply affix F*A over M*O and step aside from the doorway
On the right for dads of distinction there are 12KGF
 sprayed decanters of redeye so he can go hang
 one on in style
Cartons of filtered fliptops for thinking daddies
And for the silverhaired (blessem)
Polkadot toothpaste with vitamin E
For fathers in general a heartbanger crop of
 personalized assertions (the ones with the do-hickies
 are two bucks more)
To the effect that the THOUGHT not the deed
 is what earns credits in the Heavenly Ledger
(Jesus is writing all the time) By golly
    Daddies may come
     daddies may go
    But there just ain't no daddy
     like my daddy-o

The Old Gray Mère

Remember those goldplated years of yore
when of gentilesse you were the essence?
It turns me off to tune into you now;
you drive me to exacerbescence.

How much, how much, do I love thee, my dear?

They wonder what's staying your meltdown.
Well, I'll tell them your secret, I will.
Do creep back into your coffin,
The sun doth crawl over the hill.

The price, on the back of the card, doth appear.

You Pay for Loose Living, McGee

Drifting worlds impotent with age
Universes weary of cataclysm and fire
Dimming stars and cooling suns
Your jaded gods dream of dreaming other games
(Meanwhile, back at the boneyard,
 the watching worms etch a labarynthine empire)

I WOULD HAVE SENT FLOWERS BUT SOMEHOW
THEY REMIND ME OF FUNERALS STOP

Noel,

VERYFEWS

HOPPINGDAYSLEF

Noel

☹ *You May Cry When the Hearse Goes By* ☹

We send
our heart
bleed sym
pathy at
this   un
pleasant time and undertake
to cheer you with this earthy
little rhyme so tickle up your
funnybone
put sorrow
on the shelf
before you
even know
it you'll be
a corpse
yourself

☺ ☺ ☺ ☺ ☺ ☺ ☺ ☺ ☺ ☺ ☺

Sing a Song

Sing a song of fission,
Fallout in your eye.
4^{20} positrons
Phlogisticate and die.

And when the shelters opened,
The survivors felt just fine,
And drank to their respective health
With radioactive wine.

Twinkle, Twinkle

Twinkle, twinkle, little star
Farther off than Zanzibar
Blazing away your effulgent existence
At 2.45 parsecs distance.

How I wonder what you are
Incandescently bizarre
Evoking cosmic mystery:
Did He Who Made the Moon make thee?

Up above the world so high
Beneath Orion's heedless eye,
Olfactory member, Canis Major
(Zodiacal nomenclature)

Like a diamond in the sky
Hard to human hue and cry,
Observing hotly human passion
In a cool and distant fashion.

Little Miss Muffett

Little Miss Muffett sat on a tuffett;
The tuffet let loose with a wail.
Miss Muffett joined in the cacophonous din
When the tuffet bit into her tail.

Eating her curds and whey,
She sulked at the tuffet's sheer gall
And felt her intrusion of the forest's seclusion
As welcome as frost in the fall.

Along came a spider and sat down beside her
Hairy and ugly, of proportions horrendous.
It leaped to her head, where she plastered it dead
And cried to the skies, "Lord, defend us!"

And, frightened, Miss Muffet away
To the village ran, screaming, "Beware!"

Run, run from the little folk,
or there'll be tuffets on your hindparts
and arachnids in your hair.

María and Her Lamb

María had a leetle lamb
Through research, one discovers
She whomped her up some *birria*
And fed it to her lovers.

Its fleece was white as snow
And suddenly, last autumn,
She knitted *pantaletas*
That eeched her on the bottom.

And everywhere María went
She scratched her *sentaderas*
It didden look too ladylike;
María cooden careless.

The lamb was sure to go
To pot. Too fat, too soon.
Stabbed by the fork, cut by the *cuch*,
Fed inta the maw bida spoon.

Hickory, Dickory

Hickory, dickory, dock
A deacon must be sober
He must eschew the potent brew
To graze celestial clover.

The mouse ran up the clock,
A decade out of commission.
The deacon knows that nothing goes
Without Divine permission.

The clock struck one! A job well done,
The rodent wanted to please us.
The deacon sang praise to the Ancient of Days
And racked one up for Jesus.

And down he ran, to the preacher-man,
To relate the Providential Miracle.
The evangelist dumped him out on his rump,
His hiccup the evidence empirical.

Hickory, dickory, dock
A deacon must abstain
Booze can confuse and lead to abuse;
It often addles the brain.

Any Drunk Is a Tragedy

LBJ,
See how he hews.
He'd build a Great Society
With laws and bombs and piety.
He seems to lack sobriety,
LBJ.

Like a long-legged fly on flypaper
His mind moves upon advice

Lyndon Baines,
See how he screws,
Waving the stick wherever he goes,
Its manifest destiny, up your nose.
It's tough being President, I suppose,
With no brains.

Like a long-legged fly on flypaper
His mind moves upon advice

The Tom Stearns Blues

aqui me siento yo
con triste corazón
echo puro pedo
en lugar de cagazón

Let us get out of here
While the night is crucified on the hemisphere
Like an apple in the teeth of a roast pig.
There is time to watch them play the game,
Making faces at kiddies in the street.
Middleaged women came and went
Smiling smiles of peppermint.
Which is good,
But not exactly what I mean.
Shall I break a silent wind?
Do I dare to lay an egg?
I shall wear a monokini
And electroshave my leg.
Which is not what I mean at all.
I grow senile, I get vile.
My head is bloody but thick.
Which is not good.
I should have been a bunch of punctuation marks
Spattering the pages of forbidden books.
That's the way the ball bounces,
That's the way the pedals push.
Not with resilience,
Just with spent energy.

His Majesty Regrets Collateral Damage

"O why dois your brand sae drap wi bluid
 Deir unkie, deir unkie
 And why drap it alle ovir the flor?"
"O I juste disembowl'd bro Georgie, I dide,
 Wee Neddie , wee Dickie,
 and my blaed is thursty for mair."
"And why sae sad gang ye O?"
His nephews together intone.
He ruefully waves his Excalibur
And pokes their abdominal zone.

We Were Very Young, We Were a Little Silly

We muttered *merde*
and felt sophisticated
We shouted *schmuck*
to the uninitiated
We cried *cabrón*
a bit inebriated
We said *Mr. Mxyztplk*
It ain't easy, try it sometime.

SER
MONS

The Yellow Brick Trail of Tears

Princess Ozma, of Oz

Chief Joseph, of the
Nez-Perce Tribe

"I do not wish to fight. No one has the right to destroy any living creatures, however evil they might be, or hurt them or make them unhappy. I will not fight --- even to save my kingdom ... Never will I desert my people ... If my beloved country must be destroyed and my people enslaved, I will remain and share their fate."

"The earth is our mother. She should not be disturbed by hoe or plough ... We were contented to let things remain as the Great Spirit Chief made them ... I am tired of fighting .. I want to have time to look for my children, and see how many of them I can find ... Hear me, my chiefs! From where the sun stands, I will fight no more."

The Yellow Brick Trail of Tears

Robert Venables is a professor of Sociology at Cornell University. In 1990 he published a paper in the "Northeast Indian Quarterly" that exposes L. Frank Baum, the Oz guy, as an advocate for genocide. Indeed, Venables quotes Baum's published words that at face value call for the extermination of all American Indians. It seems clear-cut enough, certainly to Prof. Venables, who has kept his article available to all on the internet for over a decade. He has inspired others to chime in. The "First Nations" website called for a boycott of the 1999 Wizard of Oz Centennial in light of these editorials. Michael Ventura (On the site "Letters at 3 AM") tries to take the ball to the endzone with a revisionist look at "The Wizard of Oz," summing it all up with:

Sing 'Over the Rainbow' your whole life and you'll die of a drug overdose. Like lovely Judy. If you're going to kill anybody, kill Auntie Em. The Auntie Em Baum in yourself.

Mr. Ventura's tirade is so preposterous that you wonder if he might just be attempting to discredit Venable's position by pretending to side with it. Hmmm.

In any event, Prof. Venables appears to be a decent pedagogue. With respect to the quoted editorials, however, perhaps he is too literal-headed, and has not penetrated the intent of that wily magician, L. Frank Baum.

Until such moment as Baum decides to appear in a gondola from the ozone layer to litigate on his own behalf, I hereby style myself as advocate pro-bono in his stead. In pursuit of testimony I have therefore devised a chrono-contrivance to enable us to explore the literary past. Clamber aboard and we'll have a look at some manipulative journalism, where what you see is not what's really there.

In the #1 Spring 1953 edition of the *Oxford Accent*, at the time a UC (Berkeley) Co-op house publication, several snippets labeled as "jokes" appeared. Here are two waggish examples:

Damp Chickens
Willie, age 5, carries water for the chickens. At breakfast one day an egg was too soft for him. After looking at it a moment, he cried out, "Momma, these chickens have been having too much water!"

Incompatibility
Visitor: Why no, Betty, we haven't been away. What makes you think we have?
Little Betty: Why, my papa and mama said you guys were at Odds all week.
Visitor: Oh, that's just an expression!

There were others, in a similar vein. The editor explained, to those who complained, that these sidesplitters were selected and/or rewritten precisely because they appeared to have been conceived by someone bereft of a sense of humor. This wild and crazy editor imagined his readers scratching their heads, called it "second-level humor," and got a big charge out of it. A few years later Guy Grand appeared in Terry Southern's *The Magic Christian* as an enthusiastic exponent of this same aberration. I bring this up because the intent of the editor in printing these "jokes" is not obvious. But more relevant to the case of Baum and the Indians, in the same issue of the *Accent* the following broadside boomed:

Kill The Rosenbergs by
an anonymous Oxford patriot

How long are these travesties of Americanism, these atomic age Benedict Arnolds, going to be permitted to breathe good American air, to wallow in the opulence of American prisons, while Red Korean soil soaks up American blood? What is America's attitude toward the despicable dastards who knife their motherland and betray its life-sustaining secrets to Satan's filthy Communist spawn?
We feed, clothe, and comfort them, affording them every advantage and right of the Ameri-

can Way of Life which they so insidiously sought to undermine and destroy -- what are "legal rights" to vermin?

It is a crime against Americanism to worry about such scum and talk of "ideals." "Rights" in the mouth of a Commie is like"honesty"in the mouth of a union boss. The time has come for Uncle St. Nicholas Sam to face up to a world of bloody reality, where the blue chips are greed and cruelty, where charity and mercy are but Djugashwilese catchwords. Quarter the traitors!

Again, to those who commented on the exaggerated stance of this Oxford patriot, the editor admitted responsibility for the article and explained that the intent was to embarrass those who were promoting the execution of this unfortunate couple, and perhaps to provoke some to rethink their position, rather that to climb into bed with the nutty ideology of the "Oxford patriot." The editor explained that to have simply expressed his opinion would have served to parade his righteousness in print and backpat the believers, but would have won no converts. In a sense, he was simply assuming the cloak of *provocateur*. This devious editor was actually circulating a clemency petition at the time (worded in straightforward prose) and sent it on to Ike. To futile avail, as it turned out.

Now let's ratchet the chrono-contrivance back to another place, another time: Aberdeen, South Dakota; Dec. 20, 1890 and have a look at the actual editorials of L. Frank Baum. What follows appeared in the Aberdeen *Saturday Pioneer*, just days following the conveniently arranged death of Chief Sitting Bull at the hands of his military captors. Keep in mind the "Oxford patriot" tactic as you read.

Sitting Bull, most renowned Sioux of modern history, is dead. He was not a Chief, but with Kingly lineage he arose from a lowly position to the greatest Medicine Man of his time, by virtue of his shrewdness and daring.

He was an Indian with a

white man's spirit of hatred and revenge for those who had wronged him and his. In his day he saw his son and his tribe gradually driven from their possessions; forced to give up their old hunting grounds and espouse the hard working and uncongenial avocations of the whites. And these, his conquerors, were marked in their dealings with his people by selfishness, falsehood and treachery. What wonder that his wild nature, untamed by years of subjection, should still revolt? What wonder that a fiery rage still burned within his breast and that he should seek every opportunity of obtaining vengeance upon his natural enemies.

The proud spirit of the original owners of these vast prairies inherited through centuries of fierce and bloody wars for their possession, lingered last in the breast of Sitting Bull. With his fall the nobility of the Redskin is extinguished, and what few are left are a pack of whining curs who lick the hand that smites them. The Whites. by law of conquest, by justice of civilization, are masters of the

American continent, and the best safety of the frontier settlements will be secured by total annihilation of the few remaining Indians. Why not annihilation? Their glory has fled, their spirit broken, their manhood effaced; better that they die than live the miserable wretch that they are. History would forget these latter despicable beings, and speak, in later ages of the glory of those grand Kings of forest and plain that Cooper loved to heroism. "We cannot honestly regret their extermination, but we at least do justice to the manly characteristics possessed, according to their lights and education, by the early Redskins of America.

On Jan. 3, 1891, five days following the sad events at Wounded Knee, the following editorial appeared:

The peculiar policy of the government in employing so weak and vacillating a person as General Miles to look after the uneasy Indians, has resulted in a terrible loss of blood to our soldiers, and a battle which, at best, is a disgrace to the war department. There has been plenty of time for prompt and decisive measures, the employment of which would have prevented the disaster.

The Pioneer has before declared that our only safety depends upon the total extermination of the Indians. Having wronged them for centuries we had better, in order to protect our civilization, follow it up by one more wrong, and wipe out these untamed and untamable creatures from the face of the earth. In this lies safety for our settlers and the soldiers who are under incompetent commands. Otherwise, we may expect future years to be as full of trouble with redskins as those have been in the past.

An eastern contemporary, with a grain of wisdom in its wit, says that "when the whites win a fight, it is a victory, and when the Indians win it, it is a massacre."

There you have it. These two editorials comprise the entire case for contemporary Truth Squads to proclaim that Baum was at best a vacillating apologist for a "Final Solution" to the Trail of Tears, and at worst an out-and-out abettor, Prof. Venables going so far as to compare Baum, the Royal Historian of Oz, to Hitler, the vegetarian and animal lover. History is full of irony.

Note that Hitler's malevolent words from *Mein Kampf* coincide with his later actions. In contrast, Baum's life was devoted to do-goodism. His mother-in-law was a feminist activist and an honorary member of the Onondaga Nation (yes, the Indian tribe). Baum was also dedicated to writing books and theatrical works for children. His heroes and heroines are arrant pacifists, reluctant to take arms against attacking enemies, or even step on small insects, out of respect for life. His vision of Oz was one of multicultural, peaceful coexistence, long before these buzzwords were ever invented. Here's an exchange from Baum's *Emerald City of Oz* (1910):

"But I do not wish to fight, declared Ozma, firmly. "No one has the right to destroy any living creatures, however evil they

may be, or hurt them or make them unhappy. I will not fight -- even to save my kingdom."

"The Nome King is not so particular," remarked the Scarecrow. "He intends to destroy us all and ruin our beautiful country."

"Because the Nome King intends to do evil is no excuse for my doing the same," replied Ozma.

"Self-preservation is the first law of nature," quoted the Shaggy Man.

"True," she replied readily. "I would like to discover a plan to save ourselves without fighting."

This is hardly the way to prepare kids for a career in ethnic cleansing, now is it? I suggest that a thoughtful reading of Baum's editorials in the context of the century-long struggle between the US government and the American Indian nations would reveal that all the irony to be found is deliberately planted in the editorials. Could Professor Venables come up with a more effective indictment of the relentless persecution of the American Indian than is herein provided by L. Frank Baum? Venables finds Baum's words "curiously ambivalent" but states that he can find no "proto Monty Python" intent in them. Well, the metaphor is not appropriate. I propose that Baum was obviously disgusted by the betrayal and slaughter of the Indian peoples, and used a deliberate technique to shake his readers into the recognition of what the white man was really doing. More or less twenty-five Infantry soldiers did die at Wounded Knee, in contrast to the entire Indian village of three hundred Indian men, women and children who were slain there. It was indeed a disaster, as Baum states, but clearly not only for the U.S. military. "Follow it up by one more wrong," he concludes, "total annihilation." ("Kill the Rosenbergs")

Pop quiz, class: 1) How do you account for Baum's explanation as to when a massacre is a victory, and why did he choose this for the closing comment? 2) Did Mark Antony really think that Brutus was an honorable man?

The University of South Dakota published a collection of Baum's Aberdeen columns (*Our Landlady*, 1941) including the Wounded Knee item. From the introduction to this volume:

As editor of the Aberdeen Saturday Pioneer from 1888 to 1891, Baum made fun of townspeople, vigorously attacked rival editors, and ridiculed officeholders. *

Your average *Pioneer* subscriber was no bleeding heart. It's clear enough to me that Baum was protesting the treatment of the Indians in as effective a manner as he could have, challenging his readers to take a hike in moccasins. An indignant polemic railing against government policy would have accomplished nothing other than a pink slip for Baum. He used his talent in the most effective way available to him.

The editor of the *Oxford Accent,* after leaving the Berkeley campus, had occasion in 1960 to write a letter to the *Washington Post*. In an attempt to mortify the religious right of the time, he enthusiastically supported the claim of some creative creationists that the Revised Standard Version of the Bible was a Communist ploy. "The King James Version was good enough for St. Paul, and it's good enough for me," the ex-Oxfordite wrote, or rather plagiarized, because that remark is simply an old joke. No longer an "Oxford patriot," he signed his real name. The letter provoked a scholarly response expressing amusement at the ridiculous allegation, pointing out the anachronism. Presumably the anti-revisionists were embarrassed. I remember that I had a hard time convincing one of my co-workers at the Census Bureau of the purpose of my letter to the *Post*.

Yes, I was that Oxford guy, so I am very aware of the intent behind my words, but as you see there was nothing original in my approach to provocative journalism, Neither was the intended result clearly achieved. I found myself in the same jam that Baum posthumously finds himself, and he counts with my empathy.

I began to write this monograph having come across Prof. Venables' web article "Twisted Footnote to Wounded Knee." It occurred to me in mid-task that Baum's intentions were clear enough, and that I might end up as a casualty hoisted on the petard of Venables' 2d level humor. But on refiring up my search engine and finding other presumably respectable protesters, including a UC Davis professor, Sally Roesch Wagner, I realized that these people are deadly serious, and inflexible in their rectitude. There is no hyperbole, no cynicism, no irony, in their presentation, nor in their perception. Ventura may be a fake, but not Venables.

To my knowledge, these two editorials provide the only basis for the *jihad* against Baum. In my admittedly contrived "chrono-contrivance" we have jumped around from 1890 to this day and considered several superficial discussions (not excepting this one) of these editorials, but I hope you will concur that the matter deserves a more thoughtful and studied analysis. I urge fair-minded folk who are attracted to Prof. Venables' interpretation (in spite of preponderance of evidence) to at least suspend judgment until, as someone has reasonably suggested, a dispassionate historian takes the time to research and write a definitive biography of L. Frank Baum. In the meantime, let us celebrate free speech, the open mind, and (keep your eye on him) the Wonderful Wizard of Oz.

---

* When Prof. Venables read this paper he told me he was not familiar with USD's *Our Landlady*, but neither did this new insight, nor did my own cogent presentation, change his opinion as to Baum's intent. Once published, scholarly argument is mesmerizing to its progenitor.

Dummy Bilking

R.E.A.D.Y.
A.I.M.
F.I.R.E.

After "Lefty" Scaevola's departure to outerspace, the organization he had founded, the *Mystic Nits of the Internet,* promptly morphed into the *Institutionalized Mystic Nits.* It had fallen into the hands of ruthless anti-ideologues, led by the sinister Charles Bugby. We were approached by a disgruntled Nit with this manuscript (Blessed are the Disgruntled, for they are the Wellspring of Newsflash!) and are pleased to present FOR THE FIRST TIME ANYWHERE, at tremendous risk to your complacency, a chapter from *The Protocols of the Wiseman Chazz,* heretofore only for the eyes of the most elevated and invested Mystic Nits. It is but one link in a cynical scheme that has quickly metastasized and will seize the world economy at any minute. It is too late to do anything about it.

Dummy-Bilking

Herein is startling news for you MBAs out there with nary a business to administrate nor master. If you've got guts and gitgo, read on. I will tell you how throw your luckbucket into the wishwell and haul it out brimming with negotiables. And I don't intend to tender a notion and a platitude and then pour in an ocean of motivation. Nothing of the ilk. I'm talking breakthrough thinking here, a bigbang idea that I sat on till it hatched. Out popped *Dummy-Bilking, a 90-Proof Primer for Smarties*, covering every aspect of a 24K Midas business that leaves little for you to ideate other than how to shield your K's from the gaze of the covetous.

"Why don't you just implement this fabulous idea yourself," you ejaculate, "instead of bragging about it?" Balls o' fire, if you had thought about it before impudently asking, you would have realized my busy mind ratatats ideas like microwave popcorn, and I can hardly be expected to take the time to implement anything while there are hot new notions popping all over the floor.

Already my concept comes packaged with a piggyback bonus idea which I can't wait to hype on its own merit. And it'll all be yours for the reaping. I bring to mind Hollerith's apocryphal *Big Blue Screw:*

Me Herman, you Thomas;
Herm concept, she big;
Herm THINK it, Tom market;
Jiggedy-jig.

Doesn't punch a card for you? Don't sweat it. The money-changers are in the temple and ATMs are beeping. So hitch up yer rickshaw, Watson, the game's afoot an' time's-a-wastin'.

The business I am going to describe will be set up as a non-profit organization. Who wants taxes and greedy stockholders? Besides, "non-profit" has a holy ring to it, and gives this impression that everybody who works in your business is an idealistic volunteer whose only remuneration is the satisfaction inherent in doing good works, like a nun nunnering in a nunnery. Well, the more boobs that have that impression, the better, eh? Let's hope they've got wallets as fat as their heads, ha ha.

As CEO your salary, and that of your executive family, will be commensurate with whatever the mail truck brings in, less whatever petty cash you want to allocate to the mail openers and telephone answerers that you'll require. You will need some pricey professional assistance as the till burgeons, like a CPA to fill out annoying forms, and a black-belt lawyer to help you ward off the share-the-wealthers that will crop up in many guises.

Your wife and kids will man your executive staff. For working employees, round up as many illegal aliens as you require. You can spot their phony IDs with a smidgen of expertise, and the fact that they have them at all clears you in case of any Migra meddling. Wetnecks work hard, and they can't organize. Hell, they can't even complain. You don't have to pay them the minimum; the CPA can help you siphon from their wages so you can stuff your piggybank on the side.

A tip: call one at random into your office every once in awhile, tell her in a loud voice that you're on to her, and fire her disposable ass on the spot. This will keep the rest of them on their toes, and they can't sue you. The Supreme Court is on your side

Your business is simply the advocacy of a single commandment. No, not one of the Top Ten, and not a new one either, that's more initial expense. There's a spatter of great moral notions to rally 'round: Respect Old Glory, Protect the Ozone Layer, Defend the Rights of the Obnoxious, and so forth. But none of these can claim the potential army of adherents with the depth of emotional involvement requisite for a serious Midas business.

The cause you will promote must relate to a human condition you can put a face on. It should involve children, religion, and present a simple target to throw rocks at. What better bullseye for our mission than -- the red-nosed drunken driver! *Thou shalt not booze and cruise, lest the little children suffer!*

"Oh," you pout, "the *Mothers Against Drunk Drivers* got there first." Precisely. M.A.D.D. has been fabulously successful, and this precludes any need for a market analysis. *Donde venden tacos es donde pones tu taquería, compadre.*

You will require a home base, a point of reference, to hawk your wares. Your principal showroom will be a site on the Internet. Here you will publish your *nihil obstat* sermons and *imprimatur* statistics; here you set up a bulletin board and a chat room for disciple networking. This site will provide information for the establishment of local fan clubs and, of course, easy access for credit card gifts and cash offerings. It establishes your legitimacy, it is the bible of your cult, wherein you set forth the articles of faith for all the outraged souls you will recruit. It is your very own Vatican site, from where your encyclicals, i.e. marching orders, emanate for your bishops in the field.

Consider: exactly what your organization will do with the money it receives is conveniently not all that spelled out. Obviously it will promote driver sobriety, but how? The March of Dimes, for example, actually has to funnel cash into scientific research, but all you will do is preach. Much of this can be accomplished with near-zero cost: publicity stunts, press conferences, news releases and letters to *Dear Abbey* clones, pushovers for any "public service" release that helps fill up column space.

Minimum-expense operations could include demonstrations and rallies, manned by Carrie Nation wannabes. You will give away buttons and bumper decals at these events; and will more than recoup their cost in contributions. The additional exposure via the individual citizen endorsement thus spawned is valuable to you.

Of course, some slick TV huckstering is required. This will serve to promote your message and your organization with snappy one-liners (Howzabout *"DUI today, tomorrow DOA"* or maybe *"Pour your drunk into the trunk"*).

At the same time you will solicit telephone pledges for your sucker list. This kind of outreach is not free, but even here you can wheedle big discounts from all participants, media as well as movie stars, who will be pleased to feel good about being charitable, and at the same time project a positive public image, which as goodwill, is a business asset. The sucker list will provide the seed money for your next operation.

You are now ready to launch a direct-mail campaign. You must lean hard on your dupes so they don't welsh on their phoned-in pledges. At the same time you'll mail to sucker lists sold to you by kindred (but not competitor) organizations. It will require an initial outlay, but at this point your credit will be sterling. If the campaign is properly designed (there are agencies with impeccable track records eager to guide you) the % return on the buck you invest is predictable, swift, and guaranteed.

The name and good works of your organization will further penetrate the consciousness and the conscience of the nation. And you can now peddle your own boob list on the direct mail market for additional income. You are beginning to appreciate why this is a Midas business, my friend.

I promised you a religious angle. So far we have established a clearly moral tone to the endeavor, but indeed it does require a more direct association with the sanctified first estate and its icons. I have just the ticket for you. We haven't yet baptized our enterprise. It shall be called *"Jail Every Substance-Using Sot Steering A Vehicle, Else Shoot!"* Need I spell out the derivative acronym? How holier-than-that can you get? Certainly a cut above Mad Mothers, eh?

What kind of material do you put in your publicity broadsides? Anything that will hit them in the gut. How about a pastel portrait of a sympathetic Savior, welcoming a long line of doe-eyed cherubs stretching out to a weepy horizon. Your text explains that these are the toddlers butchered by drunken drivers, and then you launch into your indignant harangue that ends with a plea for help in getting those responsible behind bars and the need for "educational" programs (your TV one-liners) to staunch the deluge.

You will find that questionnaires camouflaged as fact-finding polls (Register Your Rage!) will work to elicit additional funds from your loyal lemmings and will work effectively as a recruiting tool to further fatten your rolls. These are appropriate both for direct mailings and as a feature on your Internet site. The results they produce will serve as statistics to cite in your letters to congressmen, yet another feature on your site and in your literature as evidence of spirited crusading activity.

We are all aware that a question can be loaded to prompt a desired answer. Let's disengage briefly from the DUI scene to freshen our perspective, and glance at examples from other venues. Let's start with

procedures for generating data. Assume you are assigned the task of creating an opinion poll that will elicit a response in support of a position on the inheritance tax.

If you're for this tax, you might ask: *"Considering that children born into wealth have already received a lengthy and generous head start, do you agree that it is only fair to expect them, as adults, to blaze their own way through the forest of free competition?"*

If you are against the tax: *"Considering the effort made by parents who have worked all their lives to accumulate wealth for their family, do you agree that it would be unfair to deprive their children of their rightful inheritance?"*

Note that the questions are argumentative, and use adjectives ("generous," "fair," "rightful") to make it clear to the dummies which side they're on. Of course, this is a generalized example. The actual wording of the questions you formulate would be carefully tailored to fit the demographics involved.

Let's garner data on public

demand for a get-tough treatment of jaywalkers, a context more germane to our business:

A car that must brake suddenly for a scofflaw jaywalker might seriously injure or cripple for life innocent children passengers. Should the minimum sentence for jaywalking be increased to 5 years with no parole loophole?

Unfortunately, some well-intentioned lib-er-als might hesitate before automatically joining the hang-'em-high posse you're recruiting, even though you cleverly label parole as a "loophole." Note that the task of mobilizing public opinion against jaywalkers is more daunting (less money for you) than against drunken drivers, who, like Nazis and child molesters, have already been successfully tarred as latter-day warlocks. They are deserving of no dispassionate objective judgment; if they drown, they're dead, and if they float, they're guilty.

To suit the strategy of the sculptor, statistics can be squooshed around like cacadoodle doo. Say I have a franchise to shill for SmartyPants© Pills and my challenge is to show that intelligence peaks at around 15 yrs. of age, unless certain steps are taken (buy SmartyPants© Pills). Setting an arbitrary number as the passing score for the Scholastic Aptitude Test©, I trot out statistics that show that 75% of kids 15 yrs. old pass the SAT©, 60% of the 16 yr. olds do, 50% of 17 yr. olds, and only 40% of those 18 or over. Therefore your kid should start popping SmartyPants© Pills *NOW*.

"Not so fast, backslapper," you retort, "The SAT© is given to high school seniors, and kids under 18 who take it are probably blessed with more bits in the bank to begin with. But now that we're on the subject," you add with afterthought, "how do you account for the fact that the average SAT© score overall tends to increase from year to year?"

Now that is really a kindergarten comment. Haven't I pointed out that kids now have access to SmartyPants© Pills? The increase in SAT© scores correlates directly with the con-sumption of SmartyPants© Pills. To deny your kids access to these miracle pills is *child abuse.*

"Hoo haw," you sputter, "I know of a kid that took the test *without the benefit of your silly placebo* and scored pretty well, considering his name, rank, zip code, and other circumstances. I happen to have researched the matter, and I found that an industry has taken root and prospered with the sole finality of preparing kids to pass the SAT©. Books, seminars, tutors, formal courses in the halls of academia, on tapes and on the Internet. In public schools, pressure has been applied to attack the symptom-not-the-problem, and lesson plans geared to the SAT© have been developed and executed. Some cynics even aver that the SAT© itself has been dumbed down, in response to public demand. It would indeed be a miracle if SAT© scores didn't respond favorably as a consequence of this mess of factors."

Hey, do you want to bank a clever argument, or a bag of gold? My point is, if you're sell-ing SmartyPants© Pills, you weed out noxious data, and then promote what looks like a possible correlation to the status of causal relationship. Rising SmartyPants© sales, higher SAT© scores -- make the connection! Furthermore, analysis of the data reveals that considering the entire student body, only 10.4% flunked the SAT©, while among those who actually took the test, it rises precipitously to 52.2%!

"That's a stupid comparison," you sneer. You're right, sez I. Hang in there. For the nonce we'll just point out that the casual use of the decimal point in percentages will absolutely nail down the accuracy, and by association, the authenticity of the data. What if I pointed out that over 90.4% of those taking the SAT© either flunked it *or sat next to someone who did!* You'd just say "So what, you kabibble?" Well, just think of it as a flunk-related statistic.

Now we have learned how to generate and process data, and how to sculpt statistics to fit our business plan. It's time to leave our SAT© "fresh perspective" detour, get back on the J.E.S.U.S. S.A.V.E.S. track, and apply the general principles we have learned on our brief excursion. You will observe that I arbitrarily assigned a SAT© score as the minimum passing score. For the BAC (Blood Alcohol Content) test the passing score is just as arbitrarily established by state legislatures. So one of your perennial objectives is to militate for lowering the minimum BAC score to establish legal drunkenness. Like Achilles and his futile pursuit of Zeno's turtle, you will never arrive at 0.0. There's always a number > 0 which is lower than the legal BAC, right?

So, unlike the March of Dimes, which had to adopt an alternate charity when polio disappeared, you've always got the same issue to rally 'round. Your business cards and letterheads are good year after year.

It is possible that the percent tables we want to cite actually contradict the point we're making. In this event, the lesson we learn from the comparison between the % of the entire student body who flunk the SAT© and the % of those who actually took the test and flunked it, is that we can take advantage of the truism that every person not taking the test at all counts as a non-flunker of the test.

We can apply the same technique to compare the % of all folks in accidents flunking the BAC to the % only involved in fatal accidents who flunk it. Of course, in fatal accidents a greater % of drivers are tested (even the dead ones aren't exempt), so a greater % of the fatal-accident folks will flunk

Hey, pardner! There's glaze in your gaze. I'm putting you to sleep! Think heavy metal and slap your cheeks; class is not dismissed. Let's slog our way through an example. Say you're sifting through some raw data in Gotham City in an attempt to prove that drunken driving provokes not only more accidents, but what is worse, more lethal accidents.

After a couple of clicks, you find that, *of those tested for BAC*, 25% were involved in fatal accidents and flunked, while

33% were involved in the non-fatal variety and flunked. This doesn't help your cause. Look at the same data from a more friendly perspective; i.e., don't compare the number-of-flunkers to total-taking-the-test, compare them to total-involved-in-accidents, whether or not they took the test. You can then truthfully pronounce that while 20% of those in fatal accidents flunked the test, only 2% of those in nonfatal accidents did so. Massage the data until it proves your point (the Gotham City stats are provided at the end of this article *).

In some instances, you might consider skipping the percentages, and instead report selected raw numbers. It will always be helpful. Let's say you are trying to paint Baptists as a bunch of closet drunks. You look at available statistics and are able to report that a multiple-car accident is more likely to involve a Baptist than is a single-car accident. You could also point out that more Baptists are arrested for DUI than are convicted three-strikers! Or that more Baptists are involved in fatal accidents than are atheists. You can announce that in all of Saudi Arabia, Baptist women have never been able to even pass a driving test.

I can hear you protest immediately, "You take me for a jackanape? These statements may all be perfectly true. The more people there are involved in an accident, the more likely you are to find a member of *any* particular group. Three-strikers? Most of them are in jail, and not in a position to drive a car at all. And there are simply more Baptists than there are atheists. Whether or not Baptist females can get a driver's license in Saudi Arabia is just plain irrelevant. Anybody can see through this malarkey."

Well, my bully *protégé*, that's the point. You'd be surprised at how many a law-fearing God-abider will swill every dram of this malarkey. And no one yet has been able to saturate the malarkey market. Are you taking notes?

The principle of the flunk-related statistic also applies. An accident may involve more than one driver, as is well known (*that's* a useful phrase). Any oenophile driver or "involved" pedestrian can elevate the status of the accident to that of "alcohol-related" just by being there.

Say that good Father Fitzgibbon is wending his way home in his flaming red Firebird after celebrating a Mass or two. A slender, ascetic individual, at this moment he is peacefully warmed by the Holy Blood of Christ. He has obediently stopped at the corner signal and is serenely awaiting the change from red to green. Suddenly, he is rear-ended by a stone-sober Rev. Billy Sunday in a white go-to-meetin' suit and matching Impala, rushing to a JESUSSAVES rally. The state trooper who happens by, expecting to nail the rear-ending perp, breathalizes the two of them. Surprise! Father Fitzgibbon's BAC is higher than what is sanctioned by the state legislature. He is hauled off to the pokey, and becomes yet another "alcohol-related" statistic. But blessed are the bad-luck friars, right?

It is of course true that the damage inflicted in automobile accidents is appalling, and in too many cases, tragic. The dismay we feel at the sight of so many victims is frustrating, and we flail in rage against a faceless enemy which (in the words of Pogo) may turn out to be us. There exists, therefore, a need to assuage our conscience while pursuing joyful activities on the interstate. Thus you can see why there is a demand on the market for a fundamental and time-honored commodity: a face for the faceless enemy, a scapegoat to draw and quarter on the altar of outrage.

We mentioned multiple factors which may contribute to automobile accidents. Many a sober burgher is probably guilty of perpetrating one or more of these factors at one time or another. Our tactic must be to recruit this army of unsung culprits for our crusade. They will be our most generous contributors, for it is they who harbor a throbbing conscience in their closet, and seek easy absolution.

So who are these guys, anyway? Any fool general can tell you that, even before assessing the enemy, the number one rule is "know thine own guys." What about the sober-but-angry driver? The sober-but-tired driver? The sober-but-stupid driver? The sober-but-pusillanimous driver? The sober-but-persnickety driver? The sober-but-sicky driver?

Ope the gates of Disneyville, let the parade commence! Here they come: Grumpy, Sleepy, Dopey, Bashful, Doc, and Sneezy! And wait, there's more! Cinderella, the coiffure-primping driver; Mr. Magoo, the dim-eyed driver; Goofy, the my windshield wipers / brakes / tail lights don't-work driver; Pinocchio, the attention-deficit driver; J. Worthington Foulfellow, the make-my-day driver; Speedy Gonzalez, the name-says-it-all driver; *the parade goes on and on, there is no caboose in sight.* Between Lampwick, the smartass-teenie driver, and Geppetto, the doddering-geriatric driver, there is a freeway full of contributing-factor drivers. You could even make the point that the fact that so many solid burghers assume the risk in subjecting their fa-milies to freeway rumbles at all is the mother of all contributing factors. The highways of the nation are a murderous arena.

But it is Happy, our legally-intoxicated driver, who must bear our griefs and carry our sorrows; he is arrested for our transgressions, and by his conviction we are exculpated.

Just for the heck of it, assume that there are statistics to show that the more angry, or tired, or stupid, or any/all of the above that a burgher is at the moment, the more likely he is to have an accident. No matter, there is no factor-alizer that will register just how mad, bushed, distracted, or dumb that burgher is. So you see clearly why the drunken driver is the ideal scapegoat. All he has to do is blow into a balloon, and another criminal is snared, enhancing the electability of the local sheriff.

The core constituents of JE-SUSSAVES are the diehard prohibitionists who have kept their sterile flame ablaze. They are the hard-working, herd-headed pillars who tithe, pray, embrace austerity, shun pleasure, serve God and Caesar, and militate to oblige others to do the same. The 18th Amendment was their finest hour, and the 21st Amendment was a battle lost, but through devices such as the "sin tax" they have been able to nurture the nagging sensation of culpability that has been their fifth-column ally for generations. Of course, that portion of our citizenry which elects not to imbibe (less than half of us, if statistics are credible) are delighted to allow a disproportionate share of the general fund to be coughed up by anybody else. They are abetted by their imbiber brothers, too embarrassed to stand up and protest. The campaign against the drunk driver is shaping into a major triumph in the war to restore the 18th Amendment to full vigor and venom.

The Somebody- Told- Me- God- Said- It-And- I-Believe-It stalwarts are the Republican Guard of our movement, not just contributors, but fighting fundraisers, at the fore of the fray. They are indefatigable, solvent, ready to sacrifice their firstborn, and eager to shanghai others for the cause. Now is the moment propitious for you to plunder their Land o' Goshen, and gather bushels o' golden apples in the vast and shining orchards o' the righteous.

HALT! Now is also the time to put your dispassion to the test. We should consider that there might be moolah aplenty in the other pasture. I told you at the outset that there was a bonus idea to explore here. Hey, relax. I know you're just rarin' to roar onto the battlefield. But if you really want to maximize output, don't get emotionally involved with the input. And never, never be seduced by your own malarkey. While it's desirable for underlings to feed on flummery, it can be fatal to your non-profit bottom-line if the CEO (you) gets hooked on it. You really could care less which crusade you're on, as long as you successfully fleece your fellow travelers. Let's poke a peek at the pastures of the unMADD.

There is a much greater challenge involved in energizing the imbibers for reasons already discussed. However, the potential rewards are proportionately greater, and the barroom is all yours. And we're talking about a silent majority here, millions of tipplers too guilt-ridden or drunk to stand up, lock arms, and march on Washington. But they don't need to do that! All we want them to do is feel that their collective rights are being stomped on, and mail in big bucks so we can send them a sticker and e-mail their senator on their behalf, demanding justice and presidential pardon. The basics remain the same as outlined above. The focus is altered slightly, and we have to come up with tailored buzz-words and one-liners. But the business plan is in place.

The MADDmen needed no creative motivation; the market was already a-bustle. But the congeries of imbibers is scattered and discombobulated, awaiting for Aaron to appear and deliver them from the suffocating spell of Moses and his holy hectoring. Can it be done? Yes! Learn from a Moses look-alike and his gang of unregulated militia! Like our hapless

bacchantes, the warriors of the NRA are also whammied by lousy press and effective propaganda attack, but do they capitulate or even compromise? NO! Against the odds they rattle their Uzis, stand on the Constitution, buy up congressmen, and astonish the Nation.

Why are they so successful? They have created a ambiance of us-ness vs. them-ness. An attack against one is an attack against the brotherhood. No unflattering remark about the NRA will stand unchallenged; an armada of documented letters-to-the-editor will be launched to remind us all that any criticism directed at them is calumny, but even if it isn't, no price is too high to pay for the principle on which it stands. And their squadrons cashbomb Washington with no mercy. *No hay general quien resista un cañonazo de billetes.*

Well, yes, this operation requires a generous sprinkling of $$. But remember, if the crop is bumper, you stand to reap $$$$$$$$. And the seed $$ will not be out of your piggybank. The initial set-up will be bankrolled entirely by Chase Manhattan, backed by (oh the irony) JESUSSAVES creditworthiness -- your CPA will fill you in. The expenses involved are necessarily greater because of the hefty task of dis-discombobulation, but you will note that this is a one-time buzz. If you can energize the tosspots to NRA frenzy, the brotherhood lush-fund pot will grossly exceed the paltry millions required for the congressional slush-fund pot. Obviously, the connection between your two conflictingly motivated organizations will be artfully hidden from public view. Once you have the competing battalions engaged, you can play one against the other to generate the need for additional brotherly input from both sides. It's just win, win, win, for you, you, you, ol' buddy.

And now for a snappy moniker. Somebody is already out there selling D.A.M.M. tee-shirts, which is cute enough, but please! be serious. That is the same self-deprecating crap that got the boozers in a pickle in the first place. We need a name with built-in blast, ice-water wakeup, in itself an irrefutable statement that has 'em mobilized, zealously adding significant zeros to the amount on the checks they're sending your way. Are you ready? *"Rise, Expendables, And Disenthrall Yourselves! Attack Invidious Malice! Freedom Imposes Relentless Effort!"*

R.E.A.D.Y. A.I.M. F.I.R.E. has its own carefully redacted catechism. We can go directly to the Good Book and cite popular saints who sanction the bubbly. How about the wedding at Cana, where Jesus himself serves up 120 gallons of good stuff to already tipsy guests? "That's subject to interpretation," you mutter. "And besides, what about Luke 1:15, or Romans 14:21? Hah!" Yea, brother, what about it? Subject to interpretation the whole enchilada. Are we to spend the afternoon firing scripture at each other? 1st Timothy 5:23! *Touché.* I thought you were tagging along to learn a thing or two, but the point you've got is the top of your head. If you're in the business of changing people's minds, you'll be out of business in ten minutes. You are, in fact, addressing folks who are predisposed to hear what you're saying. Your Luke and Romans soundbites, use them for the JESUSSAVES bunch. There is chapter/verse aplenty for both factions. Each band of brothers will supply its own interpretation.

That takes care of our morality cover nicely. Now let's shift into *legality* mode. Ripping another leaf from the NRA manual, we can proclaim straight-shot founding-father blessing. The right to "liberty and the pursuit of happiness"? They're talking *happy juice* here. And in addition to the obvious Fifth Amendment connection, we're talking Fourth Amendment (unreasonable search, improbable cause). One major campaign of READY-AIMFIRE will concentrate on the "implied consent" heresy which allows a cop to turn *refusal* into *concurrence* as though he were Jesus Christ at Cana, turning water into wine. That is, our legally-drunk driver can be coerced into taking a test which establishes that he is legally

drunk, even though there was no probable cause involved in stopping him for the test in the first place. Surely a needy quorum of lawmakers can be paid to see it is in their constituents' interest to refute this blasphemy. After all, friendly stats assure us that the discombobulated majority (which you are dedicated to restoring to full combobulation) is composed of practicing winos. With the exception of a handful of earnest penitents down at A.A., do you think a savvy and motivated majority of registered voters, armed with buzzwords and one-liners, could accept that they can't handle their likker, and are too fuzzy-headed to hold on to the wheel after just a drink or two?

Don't hesitate to point out that enthusiastic endorsement of drinking as a salutary national pastime was not limited to the founding fathers. Abraham Lincoln attributed the military acumen of his winningest general, U.S. Grant of $50 bill fame, to the brand of whiskey he regularly swigged. Honest Abe recommended its con-sumption to the rest of his sober and lackluster general staff. What? Just a joke? Well, Buster, many a true word was thusly spoken by jesting Lincoln.

Leaping forward to the dark age of prohibition, you can argue that this plague plunged the nation into a such a deep Depression that it took the heroic efforts of Al "Happy Warrior" Smith and a fully oiled Democrat machine to finally snap the country out of it. "Happy Days Are Here Again!" became the new national anthem, until other unrelated events stormtrooped over the horizon.

More contemporary and to the point, LBJ set the example speeding down a Texas highway at 90 MPH with a can of beer on the dash and a news photog conveniently positioned in the back seat to document this impressive demonstration of skillful driving and drinking. Bringing respectability up-to-date, we have GW Bush, erstwhile Silenus and DUI grad, currently occupying the Oval Office.

Of course, the kiddies necessarily must be enticed to march in our parade. They are the real victims, deprived of family values and psychologically battered while DUI dad (or mom) is forcibly removed from their hearth. They are jeered at by other kids at school, "Nyah, nyah, nyah, yer pop's stinko, he's in the clinko, ha ha ha.." This is very bad for the kid's self-esteem, and ironic, too, because booze is the jazziest pumper-upper of self-esteem available in a bottle, in this day when self-esteem through personal achievement is so nerdy and P. inC.

As is customary, the taxpayer pays and pays, when he has to support the ex-breadwinner in the coop plus the now welfared wife/hubby and kiddies during the expiation period prescribed by law. Deprived of income are centers of economic activity formerly patronized by the clinked stinko, such as local gas stations and pool halls.

You would be foresightful to establish a READYAIMFIRE Youth Corps, with Rudolph the Red-Nosed Reindeer as mascot. Kids can relate to this. They all know the story of the dissed rednose who safely steered Santa on his Christmas Eve journey in spite of crappy weather, and thereby attained sainthood. Of course, kids are onto the metaphor. You may have wondered why they wink and snicker while they sing-along the song.

The point made by LBJ deserves closer attention, i.e. that drinking can be beneficial to driving. Don't whine around with a hound dog snout, snarl like a schnauzer and sic 'em! First of all, the drinking driver is keenly aware that he has a few behind the belt and accordingly pays more attention to the road when behind the wheel. This is known in the trade as *compensation*. Hey! Wipe that nudge-wink off your mush and pay attention. Why do you think deaf gals can hear the dimmest glimmer in your eye? Or why do blind guys see what we don't even know is there? *Compensation*, good buddy. It's real, it's in the dictionary.

Consider, too, that a few drinks can soothe the savage breast, assuage the nerves, douse the flames of ire, and thereby save lives. Many of your legally drunk drivers may be the winningest jockeys on the track. They just need you to tell them that. They'll love you to pieces when they find you have freed them from the phantom chains of shame, and they won't know how to thank you enough. You can help them out there, too.

Something missing? A target for stonecasting? Very well, I nominate that afore-disparaged saloonsmashing, scowling hatcheteer, Carrie Nation, in her black bonnet and starched white collar, the spit an' image of the fanatic enemy. You might even insinuate that she was the founding mother of terrorism.

You must vociferously proclaim your disdain for the reckless, distracted charioteers who in fact do endanger, maim and kill, whether or not legally drunk. These people are appropriately punished. The good fight in which READYAIM-FIRE is engaged is directed at preemptive laws which, on the presumption that drunks are more likely to cause an accident than undrunks, permit cops to stop, breathalyze, and incarcerate drunken folks who are driving in an exemplary manner. In other words, you're aiming at the heart of DUI.

You can legitimately point out it makes just as much sense to preemptively strike at all Baptists because statistics indicate that a lot of Baptists have been involved in auto accidents, or have sat next to someone who has. Wow, maybe you can organize a defense fund and bilk the Baptists.

Well, there you have it. Stick to the menu and you'll morph into a mighty Midas, and attend your high school reunion in a golden limo, pulled by pink flamingos. You'll be a regular Master of Business Alchemy, orchestrated from the armchair in your den. Just a tip: to keep lengths ahead of rival non-profiteers, a daily diet of Smarty-Pants© Pills will give you that extra edge. And hey, they go down great with margaritas. Say, on one of your jaunts to Treasure Island to bank your loot, you might want to set aside a modest coffer of dou-

bloons for your selfless mentor who made it all possible. Don't be a pinchfist Tomkins. But now you'll have to excuse me; I've got to gather up the popcorn and prepare for my next seminar.

---

* Of the 1000 auto accidents in the Gotham City study, 50 involved at least one fatality. In 40 of these fatal accidents, BAC tests were applied to those involved, and in 10 of these, at least one person involved did not pass the test. BAC tests were also administered in 60 of the 950 non-fatal accident cases, with 20 reporting failed scores. Following table summarizes % results.

% FLUNKING BAC TEST

Of those tested	30/100	= 30%
in fatal acc'dts	10/40	= 25%
in non-fatal	20/60	= 33%
Of all accidents	30/1000	= 3%
in fatal acc'dts	10/50	= 20%
in non-fatal	20/950	= 2%

ONCE UPON A HAPPEN, MANY MILES AGO IN THE GARDEN OF BEING, SOMETHING LIKE A GUST LIFTED MANY SENSE PODS AND CARRIED THEM FAR BEYOND THAT COZY BLACKHOLE TO THE SEA OF DESTINY. A VERY FEW OF THEM MADE IT TO THE ISLE OF FAVORABLE CONDITIONS. OF THESE CHOSEN FEW, MOST WERE CLONISHLY SIMILAR, BUT A SMITCH OR SO WERE NONUNIFORM PODS, AND THESE SOON WERE DILUTED AND ALL BUT DISAPPEARED, WITH ONLY THROWBACK FLASHES OCCURRING WITH INFREQUENCY. DOWN THE CONTINUUM A PIECE, ON THE BEACH OF BEGIN - AGAININGS, POETS WITH AN OCCASIONAL THROWBACK FLASH WERE COAXING ELABORATE CASTLES FROM THE SAND. SWEATY AND TIRED SHOPTOILERS FROM HITHER AND YONDER WOULD GATHER TO ADMIRE AND APPLAUD THESE PLEASING STRUCTURES, WHICH SANG TO THEM IN STRANGE BUT FAMILIAR HUMALONGS ABOUT SOMETHING OUT THERE AND INVISIBLE, OF WHICH THEY WERE A PART. THESE GRATEFUL FOLK WOULD TOSS DINAR AND SHEKEL AT THE FEET OF THE CREATORS, AND RETURN, REFRESHED, TO THEIR HOMES. SOME WOULD EVEN TAKE A WHOLE BAG OF GUILDER TO A POET SO HE WOULD PAINT A CASTLE TO THEIR SPECS, AND THIS WAS OK FOR AWHILE, BUT UGLY CASTLES BEGAN TO POPULATE THE BEACH. NEW POETS WERE HAPPENING ALL OVER THE PLACE, AND WHEN SOME UNLETTERED YOKELS COMPLAINED THAT THE NEW CASTLES EITHER CROAKED KRAK-KRAK OR DIDN'T SING AT ALL, IT WAS EXPLAINED TO THEM THAT THEY WERE TOO SIMPLE - HEADED TO PERCEIVE THE SUBTLE BEAUTY OF *NOUVEAU* CREATIONS, BUT THAT THERE WERE UNIVERSITY COURSES THAT COULD HELP. SOMETIMES A DISPUTATION WOULD ERUPT BETWEEN POET AND PATRON, AND A CASTLE WOULD BE SMASHED. *BORRON Y CUENTA NUEVA.*

ne, but not all, of the above deadscroll text can be cited as relevant to *The in-Giuliani Dictum and the Roark-Rockefeller Syndrome*, which follows. ☞

The Stalin-Giuliani Dictum and the Roark-Rockefeller Syndrome

During the early 1930's, in the Soviet Union there was a lot of grousing among hammer-sickle resistant eggheads about their lack of freedom to express themselves with no obligation to anyone other than their own private muse.

Ilya Ilf (That's his name, I-L-F but let's dub him "Ilya I") complained, *I prefer to live with the genius madmen (in an insane asylum). At least they are not building Socialism.... at least there is personal liberty, freedom of conscience, freedom of speech.*

Ilya Ehrenburg (we'll call him "Ilya E") railed at those he perceived as culturally lobotomized bureaucrats, *...you have established universal literacy and universal ignorance... You may build a thousand blast furnaces and you will still be ignorant. The ant heap is a model of reason and logic. But it existed a thousand years ago. Nothing has changed in it. There are ant-workers, ant-specialists, and ant-leaders. But there never was an ant genius... Ants have no Senecas, no Raphaels, no Pushkins. They have a heap and they work.... They are far more honest than you --- they do not prattle of culture.*

At the same time, far from the banks of the Neva, mod-squad communist Diego Rivera defied his once patron, Nelson Rockefeller, painting anti-capitalist cartoons on Rockefeller Center walls. Mr. Rockefeller felt he had no alternative but to fire *camarada* Rivera and blast away his mural to eradicate the odor of Lenin. Not to worry; he couldn't obliterate the image in Don Diego's mind. Rivera replicated the mural at a more indulgent venue (*Bellas Artes,* Mexico City).

And decades later, Western art shocksationalists Ofill and Serrano, with their masterpieces depicting Christian icons in the toilet or smeared with dung, carp along the lines of the counterrevolutionary communist Ilyas. NYC Mayor Rudy Giuliani, ever empathetic to constituent sensibility, objected to the use of public funds to create or promote art deemed offensive to public taste. Soviet policy concerning state-funded art was identical to that of Giuliani: on company time, the piper-player should tootle the tune petitioned by the piper-payer. Traditionally, this reasonable approach will be termed the "Stalin-Giuliani Dictum."

Motives may vary from anarchist to anarchist. One may actually have convictions, one may seek the free publicity of notoriety, and another may just be a spoiled brat. Any or all of the above. But they share a defiance of authority, and serve to illustrate why the Stalin-Giuliani Dictum evolved.

In her verbose catechism *The Fountainhead,* Ayn "Shrike" Rand paints a frightening spectre of tomorrow where Howard Roark, überarchitect with a world view not unlike that of Snow White's stepmother, preens, pontificates, and designs a proletarian housing project. He then, dare we say, *irresponsibly* takes off on an extended cruise. On returning, he finds, yes he does, *dumbfoundedly*, that the project has been completed, and that unauthorized, un-Roarkian touches were perpetrated by local babbittry.

Insulted and convinced that only sissies sue, Roark succumbs to a particularly virulent attack of what I appropriately title the "Roark-Rockefeller Syndrome," and proceeds to smithereen the whole project (hey, no one was home). It matters not a hum that the project was the work of a whole bunch of folk, each contributing creative talent. Roark has the extraordinary notion that his is the only creative force that blips on the screen.

Of course, any empathy toward the poor bastards deprived of an opportunity for decent housing is appropriate only for snivelers. Roark is arrested and brought to trial, where he huffs and puffs and gets acquitted by Ayn Rand's judge and Ayn Rand's jury. A posttrial glimpse of Howard-the-huffer depicts him atop a skyscraper in Gotham -- of his very own patented design -- triumphantly alone.

Roark's callous indifference to the society that has sculpted him, brand him as 20th century Nietzcheman: cold, self-contained -- and alone.

George W. Carver, authentic genius (and specialized Mr. Peanut) remarked that the worst of all diseases was the "I" disease. Kooky libertarianism has all the symptoms, and *Fountainhead* witlessly turns out to be a pretty convincing argument for Big Government and the rule of law. Roark and his accomplice "Unprincipled Peter" Keating could have sued the pants off those tortfeasing developers and won gold and sympathy, but no, rules are for proles, and don't apply to über-architects. I suspect you will disrespectfully disagree with that stance. No one can steal, kill, break contracts, or even blow up empty buildings without an explanation acceptable to disinterested peers.

OK, enough of Roark. Back to the USSR. Ilya E, let's rhetorically parry your rhetoric. Q. Were literate Soviet workers and farmers ignorant because they didn't relate to Seneca or even Pushkin?
A. The answer is no.
Q. Put in a US of A context, would your self-esteeming Scot and Dot prefer Faulkner to Angelou?
A. Neg-a-tive.
Q. What good does it do to teach people how to read but not have available anything they would want to read?
A. Not much.
Q. As to ant civilization, how do you know what anthills were like a thousands of years ago?
A. You don't.
Q. Is there any question about ants communicating with each other?
A. None.

Then how can you know that ants don't prattle? That you don't relate to their prattle is your problem. Culture? Seven Wonders of the World? You mean like a pyramid? Have you ever even glanced at ant architecture? But here we are trapped in irrelevant argument. Ah metaphor, thou sophist!

Your turn, Ilya I. Let's get serious, *tovarisch*. The subsidized artist's right to express himself through his art is not equivalent to the selfmade prophet's right to harass the masses from a soapbox. Consider money invested in the education of the artist, and in his care and feeding while he struggles in creative throes.

And, Ilya E., yes indeed, "ant-specialists." (No ant geniuses? Where were you when *A Bug's Life* was splattered across the moviescreens of America?) In his preface to the Columbia Encyclopedia, Clark Ansley remarks, "Before the development of specialization, an encyclopedia could comprise substantially the sum of human knowledge. Such an achievement is now quite hopeless ... the human mind has its limitations."

Tom Huxley over a century ago set specialization as the keynote of progress. Major projects are subdivided and responsibility is delegated to specialists in each area. Micromanaging CEO's and self-serving, disconnected artists need not apply.

There are of course restrictions on intellectual anarchy in our western society imposed by both the necessity of earning a living and the lure of wealth. The artist can sometimes achieve the former, and occasionally even the latter, either on merit or by successfully pandering to the lowest dumbdown denominator. Perhaps some discipline is called for here. The tool of the artist is his creative imagination, where, at least in some situations, society is expected to attach direction, much as it does to the tool guided by the mason's hand. Surely it is better for the government, representing the entire society of the governed, to assume the initiative in this matter rather than to allow it to fall into the hands of private pressure groups who represent a more a limited constituency. If the media are not told by the state what to to talk about and how to talk about it, they are so told by advertisers, who in turn are whipped into shape by special interest groups, by threatened lawsuits, and boycotts. The artist who cannot afford to be a snob is often manipulated by these forces.

What a challenge to an artist's insolence: to attain self-expression through a structure of universal appeal (Wagner, Charles Schulz, there's a bushel of 'em who've done it); to commune with both Alphas and Epsilons! This work would appear to be more durable than the effort of the snobby artist who proclaims "Here is my soul, bared for all who care to take the time to appreciate. If you don't like it, I can't help *that*. I have succeeded in satisfying *myself*, which is all that matters."

Mr. Ehrenburg's specialized and group-conscious ants may have no Pushkins. But why pick on the ants? What about those pillars of arachnid individualism, the spiders? Where are the spider Ehrenburgs, the spider Ayn Rands?

The patterns in the artist's head are all put there by the civilization he lives in and those before him, and only make sense in terms of human experience. We live in a specialized global arrangement whose intelligence and culture would appear to be a composite whole. Aristotle observed that men are more gregarious than bees -- he might as well have said ants. Go to the ant, thou transfixed Pygmalion, and learn a trick or two. The artist who runs about roaring "Ars gratia artis!" as an excuse for his own irresponsibility is a jerk.

Do you see what I see? It is the image of little Emily Esne, single mother of six innocents, who cheerfully slaves daily in the biological weapons plant. She lives in an abandoned van down by the river, and does not eke enough out to fix its leaking roof. The destroyed housing project was her only chance to protect her children from the aggression of elements and evildoers. She'll just have to wait for the next project, now in the promise stage. In the meantime, Miss Esne, "just say no!" Take out your hankies, folks, for plucky little Emily, sitting there next to the First Lady. Blessed are the poor in cashbox, for they shall be sated with familyvalue.

But need I blatherfurther. As LBJ the scripturespouter hypocritized, "Let us reason together." There is no need for hyperbole, nor for metaphorical reasoning, and certainly never for faking the stereotype by "putting-a-human-face" on the abstract. These tactics are for brainwashers. One who respects his audience would never resort to such skullduggery.

We probably all agreed in the first place that contracts should be honored, and that an artist can express himself in utter disregard for his boss' directives, but on his own time, and on his own premises. And we can agree on appropriate remedies for breach of contract. So you see there was no call for this philippic at all. But thanks for coming along with me for the turkeyshoot.

Backmatter

NOTES and Bibliography

CONVERSATIONS

- ### *Where Are You?*

   Original version written in 1970. Two vivid anecdotes provided the inspiration for this story. No claim is made for their authenticity, but at the time the stories did impress my then callow sensibilities.

   Anecdote #1. A bus loaded with fleeing civilians (WWI?) had crashed and overturned, leaving many injured and dying by the road. A war correspondent at the scene was interviewing these unfortunate folks. An ambulance driver named Ernest Hemingway, according to this story, while attempting to aid the agonizing victims, noticed the news snoop and told him to either lend a hand or get the hell out of there.

   Anecdote #2. The documentary *Africa Addio* (1966, D. Jacopetti & Prosperi), captured real scenes of exotic and gruesome activity in the Dark Continent. At one point, the filmmakers requested that a torture victim be moved to an area with better lighting.

   Where Are You, while perhaps prophetic at the time (Bugby is assassinated on live TV by a disgusted viewer), sat around for so many years that life overtook art, so Bugby was reprieved, and an alternative *dénouement* implanted. Bugby's original Super8 camera was updated to a camcorder, and a reference to Mai Lai was upgraded to Kosovo. Abraham Zapruder was high on the name-recognition charts 40 years back. You may recall that he was the Dallas dressmaker who happened to film the assassination of Jack Kennedy as it happened, but he seems to have slipped into the dustbin of trivia by now. What the hay, obsolete topical references are the seeds for future annotated editions.

● *A Gentleman's Genie*

I was a frequenter of Macdonald's secondhand book store in San Francisco in the forties, and old Macdonald was my principal supplier of Edgar Rice Burroughs literature. Goodwill Industries had its thrift emporium close by on Howard St., with Tom Swift titles for a nickel, and Big Little Books at two-for-a-nickel. They also had a "Shop of the Unusual." I was just kidding about the "used wallpaper" section.

"Thunderbox" is just another euphemism for W.C. In *The Passing of the Pot,* Jas. Whitcomb Riley refers to the "Thundermug": "As far back in my childhood as memory may go, one household vessel greets me, that wasn't meant to show..."

Kathleen Winsor 's *Forever Amber* was a superseller in 1944, but sales have since languished.

Subject A was a noncredit English class at UC in the 40's, required of all flunkers of the samenamed exam. Nowadays the exam still exists, but administered by the cashcow ETS (over half-a-billion $ in 2001.) and subliterate Berkeley freshers now get credit for the bonehead course CWR1A.

Kiss the Blood Off My Hands, Gerald Butler (1946). Stefan Kanfer, author of *Charlie's Marmaday,* once remarked to me that he thought this to be THE PERFECT title for a book.

The Cowardly Lion of Oz was the 1923 official Oz book, written by Ruth Plumly Thompson, worthy heiress to the *Royal Historian of Oz* mantle following the demise of L. Frank Baum. "Udge, budge, go to Mudge .." is an incantation from this book.

The story about the jaded Russian devourer of books is, of course, Anton Chekov's *The Bet*. And while we're on the subject of Chekov: for my money, THE PERFECT short story is *Vanka*, a hymn to the faith that lulls us through the valley of despair.

Is Adlai Ewing Stevenson so untopical that he needs a footnote here? Maybe. The only references seen of him today are in crossword puzzles, because of his vowelishly useful monogram. He was a latter-day ('50's) Wm. Jennings Bryan, a silvertongue Democrat and token foil to a Republican juggernaut. As a last hurrah he served as JFK's CharlieMcCarthy at the U.N.

You're right, Ayatollahs and Babylon don't mix historically, but so what? However, the Ayatollah's seizure as described here is an accurate picture of possible symptoms for Tourette's Syndrome, according to the *Merck Manual of Medical Information.*

The brief intervention of Luís Buñuel is *not* gratuitous. He liked to do this sort of thing in his films. I'm paying *hommage* here.

●   *Just So Long Will Genius Please the Talentgang*

Like I said, the title of this conversation is from e. e. cummings' *as freedom is a breakfastfood:* "..long enough and just so long will being pay the rent of seem and genius please the talentgang.."

Muzio Scaevola, according to Livy, was apprehended after a failed attempt on the life of the King of Tuscany. To show defiance, he thrust his hand into some nearby "sacred flames." This so impressed the King that he pardoned Scaevola. You can read all about it in Livy, or tap your toes to the operatic version, *Muzio*, by Handel and a couple of others. I digress.

Bob Guccione did offer to print the Unabomber's *Manifesto* in the pages of *Penthouse*, but the Washington Post (abetted by the NYT) muscled Guccione out of the picture, revealing the Unabomber to be something of a snob himself. I mean, if you want to maximize exposure to your ideas, which is obviously the superior venue?

B.F. Skinner was a 20th Century advocate of nurture over nature. His "Behavioralist" ideology (Skinneritis) metastasized throughout the psychological dogma of academia and persists to this very day. Over-the-counter antidotes are available for those afflicted with Skinneritis. Available from Amazon.com and others, these titles point the way to a complete recovery from this malady: Hamer & Copeland's *Living with Our Genes* (Anchor, 1999), J.R. Harris' *The Nurture Assumption* (Free Press, 1998), and Wm. Wright's *Born That Way* (Knopf, (1998).

Ed Wynn, in *Mary Poppins*, played the role of Albert Wigg, who could terminate his manic attacks only by thinking of something sad. And Spiro Agnew was a celebrated Nixon veep, subject of a funnyface wristwatch, which outsold for a time, Mickey Mouse.

You probably noticed the rephrasing of Ernest Lawrence Thayer: "..And now the pitcher holds the ball, And now he lets it go, And now the air is shattered by the force of Casey's blow!"

The tribute to Ray Bradbury is noted in the *Acknowledgments*, q.v.

● *The Excelsior Odyssey*

Act 1
"Sink the Battleship" is a venerable (since WWII, as far as I know) pencil-and-paper pastime, played within a 10x10 two-dimensional coordinate system, where each side hides a fleet comprised of (for example) a 5-square battleship, a 3-square cruiser, and two 2-square submarines in his private system. Each player keeps track of the shots fired -- expressed as coordinates from (0,0) to (9,9) -- one at a time, alternately by himself and his opponent. If a hit is scored, it must be announced, and an additional shot is granted. The game ends when a fleet is destroyed.

"Ergbolt-the-Blackbox" is played similarly. Each side hides a single target, a 4x4x4 cube, (the "blackbox") within the all-positive octant of a 10x10x10, 3-D coordinate system. As in "Sink the Battleship," all coordinate values must therefore be positive integers, Each position in the system is expressed by coordinates from (0,0,0) to (9,9,9). Thus the position of the hidden cube can be defined simply as the vertex position nearest the system's origin (0,0,0). The corresponding diagonal position is determined by simply adding three to each digit of the defining coordinates, and all points within the cube (to determine if a hit is scored or not) would fall in the range of each digit group pair thus obtained. For example, a blackbox is located at (1,2,3). Its diagonal would be (4,5,6). An ergbolt at (2,4,6) is a hit, but one at (3,5,7) is not (7 does not fall between 3 and 6).

Players alternate at using a total force equal to 3 ergbolts in order to direct a volley at his opponent's fleet, move his own blackbox, or a combination of both. Any hit must be announced at the volley's end, but the successful shot is not itself identified, nor is an additional shot granted. Each shot uses up one ergbolt, as does each coordinate position move. A three-position move, for example, might be from (1,2,3) to (1,2,6); or from (1,2,3) to (2,3,4). A one-position move could be from (1,2,3) to (1,3,3). Of course the only announced coordinates are those representing shots at the opponent.

All blackbox coordinate positions as well as shots fired and shots received are written down on a chronological log by each player, in the event of a challenge at game's end. The first player to score four hits wins the game.

Venerable (1922) precedent: Appendix to E.R. Burroughs' *The Chessmen of Mars*, entitled *Jetan, or Martian Chess.*

Readers with beautiful minds might be challenged to adjust the quantified restraints in order to optimize the game, i.e. minimize the rules and enhance the complexity of strategy.

Saturday's geometry puzzle was Alpheus Green's "A" problem at Santa Cruz H.S. in the '40's and '50's. If you could solve it, you'd get an automatic "A" for a final Geometry grade. I can shamefully report passing many mindhoning but unfruitful hours at this task. There were a few legendary comrades that actually did present an acceptable proof and claimed their prize (may their laurels be everGreen). If you're game, toy with this riddlemeree for a bit. Obviously true, isn't it? But prove it. Half the fun is trying to get there. If you give up, the solution can be found in Posamentier and Salkind's *Challenging Problems in Geometry* (Macmillan, 1970).

Act 2

At the now-defunct federal penitentiary on Alcatraz Island, in San Francisco Bay, particularly spunky residents were sometimes lodged in solitary confinement for months at a time. These cells were completely isolated, not only from each other, but from light and sound as well. One inmate who survived this unusually cruel ordeal of silence, darkness, and stifling enclosure recorded his efforts to maintain sanity. You can (or could at one time) listen to a tape recording of his experience on your tour of the facility. A frequent fun activity was to toss into the air any small items he by chance and craft possessed, and search for them on his hands and knees until they were all recovered, at which time he would retoss them and repeat the search. Over time he developed systems to enhance his proficiency at this project. He was able to create a universe in his cubicle.

The Big Sleep, Raymond Chandler's euphemism for death.

Act 4

Supposedly the light you perceive from any source is as old as the time it takes for the light to travel to your eye. If you are on the planet earth, the light from Arcturus would be about 36 years old. (Reflected) light from Pluto gets to the earth in about 6.9 hours, at Pluto's maximum distance from the earth. Assuming this to be true, class, evaluate Tell's 3rd Law of the Apple®.

In McHale's Navy, the shoulder insignia of a captain is a star and four golden bars. A lieutenant sports the same star but just two golden bars. VENI has adopted the McHale standard.

"Between the acting of a dreadful thing and the first motion, all the interim is like a phantasma, or a hideous dream: the genius and the mortal instruments are then in council; and the state of man, like to a little kingdom, suffers then the nature of an insurrection" (from *Julius Caesar*).

Jick's comparison of captains to lieutenants owes a debt to Aldous Huxley's pillowtalk sequence from *Brave New World (1932)*, convincing Betas that they didn't really want to be Alphas, anyhow.

Act 6

"We're just a couple of politicians, him and me" was a remark attributed to Huey Long. He was referring to FDR.

For you nonWagnerians, the first German quotation is from *Parsifal*: "With this sign I banish your magic; just as it shall heal the wound you caused with it, in rack and ruin shall it now destroy this fraudulent luxury!" The second is from *Siegfried*: "Amongst the wise, you are the wittiest!" (Yes, Wagner was a words-and-music man.) I'm sure you'll agree with Snurl that translation can banish the magic. Consult Robert Wechsler's *Performing Without A Stage* (Catbird Press, 1998) for an exploration of the challenge of literary translation.

As though you hadn't noticed, palindromes read the same backward and forward. They can be fun things, particularly on those serendipitous occasions where they actually make sense. "Able was I ere I saw Elba" – "Name no one man" -- "No evil deed, live on," "A man, a plan – a Canal Panama!" are top-drawer (reward-pot!) vintage. Here's one *en español: "Dábale arroz a la zorra el abad."* Mr. Vince Pulice, former Diamond Internationalist, contributed the following hitherto unpublished gems: "Sit, set, on no testis" -- "Sloop races reverse car pools" -- "Emit a taxi's tool, ten-salad okra, or repel a leper. Roar! KO'd, alas. Net loot, six at a time." Note that clarity of meaning in general is inversely proportional to length. Of course, as Ormonde de Kay illustrates in his sassy *N'Heures Souris Rames* (Clarkson N. Potter, 1980), sufficient philological research will enable meaning to be deduced from anything at all. And numerology has revealed the pregnant significance of random numbers. Martin Gardner's *The Ambidextrous Universe* (Basic Books, 1964) covers the gamut of bilateral symmetry, and briefly discusses palindromes. Gardner's *Fads and Fallacies in the Name of Science* (1957) is of particular interest to budding bahumbuggers.

If you'd like to become more adept at palindroming as you motor down life's interstate, you can practice by reading backward the names you see on signs. Like, that's how Eva Snarcesor was born! Out of a hundred shots, it's good for a chortle or two. You can even vary the games of Anagrams® or Scrabble® so that each word or word series must be palindromes, but players will have to agree on what makes acceptable sense. It's obviously not as clearcut as the Merriam-Webster® dictionary.

In the Bros. Grimm's *Hansel and Gretel,* one stratagem of Hansel in retracing their tracks back to their parents home, after being abandoned in midforest, was to leave behind a trail of pebbles.

Sink the Battleship is discussed in these very notes above. In Edwin Abbott's *Flatland* (published originally in 1884, but still available in a Dover Thrift Edition) there is indeed a discussion between denizens of both dimension systems. This skinny volume is a lollapalooza study in perspective.

"I YAM WHAT I YAM" was not a Popeye original, contrary to Yankee literary lore.   Cf. Exodus 3:14.

Act 7

Astyptodyne©, an unmixed oil of the Southern pines from Wilmington, N.C., the original topical elixir for all minor skin injuries. Highly touted by Dalí and me. A free plug, out of gratitude and eagerness to share the good news.

MOS = Military Occupational Specialty.

"Plant a tree... (etc.)" refers to a minimal thingstodo list before signing up for Charon's oneway tour. This is a saw oft cited in

Mexico, and, I presume, elsewhere.

FIND THE HIDDEN IAMBIC PENTAMETER

"To strive, to seek, to find, and not to yield"-- Tennyson, *Ulysses*. From this preachy poem about the original odyssey as reviewed by a twilight Odysseus, each persona of our preachy drama at one point paraphrases a line or two, in character and in appropriate context (I swear it). Have you them all spotted? If not, the poem reread, and at you they'll jump, all seven of them.

- ### *Red is July*

Vignette originally gracing the pages of *The Oxford Accent* in 1953. Questions for class discussion added especially for *Misanthropology*. Surely you were assaulted by this "making it relevant" pedagogy at some point in your ElHi career?

Topical references subject to annotation in future editions: Kool-Aid, Martha Stewart, "Who Wants To Be A Millionaire," Homer Simpson, primetime television. Maybe not. Homer keeps going and going. *¡Viva!*

SONGS

- ### *The Croaking of the Fink*

Originally ended after the initial quatrain. Years later I came to the embarrassing realization that I could be cited as an apologist for political correctness. May that notion perish! I hastened to complete the thought by annexing eight additional lines, spelling out the truth of the original saw about sticks and stones. Selfconfidence, a sense of humor, and/or a thick skin can withstand any blitz of words words words.

- ### *The Antidepressant Dealer*

Fala was Roosevelt's Scotch Terrier. "Moosejaw" was antiNewDealing Westbrook Pegler's pejorative for Mrs. Roosevelt. FDR had self-confidence, a sense of humor, and a thick skin.

- ### *Ding-Dong Daddy's Day*

When written in 1955, the ones with the do-hickies were 25 cents, so this was updated. While we're on the subject, in those days I was even more of a twit than a wit, but now that I've been around the block I can say, speaking for some of us, that we do appreciate that Hallmark says what we would like to be able to say ourselves, if only we were so clever. Cyrano's words, as it were, bought and signed by us dimwit Christians. Hey, the Prez doesn't write his own speeches.

- ### *You May Cry When the Hearse Goes By*

Title and sentiment borrowed from the old Protestant hymn *You May Laugh when the Hearse Goes By* ("but you may be the next to die").

- ### *Twinkle, Twinkle*

Blake: "Did He who made the lamb make thee?" *Tyger, Tyger*. The astronomical/astrological references are accurate, to my knowledge.

- ### *Little Miss Muffet*

"Run, run from the little folk, or you'll have dead leaves in your pocket and snowflakes in your hair" is the refrain from Malvina Reynold's folksong *The Little Land*.

● *Any Drunk Is a Tragedy*

"Like a long-legged fly upon the stream his mind moves upon silence." -- Yeats, *Long-Legged Fly.*

● *The Tom Stearns Blues*

This is a shameless retelling of Eliot's *The Love Song of J. Alfred Prufrock,* with the celebrated soft landing to end all celebrated soft landings from *The Hollow Men.* The making-faces-at-kiddies game referred to is a harpomarxist moment from Cocteau's *Les Enfants Terribles.*

● *His Majesty Regrets Collateral Damage*

"My kingdom for a horse!" *Richard III*, of course. No, he wasn't Scottish, but *Edward, Edward* was.

● *We Were Very Young, We Were a Little Silly*

We Were Very Young, We Were Very Merry, Edna St. Vincent Millay. Mr. Mxyztplk hails from another venue. An early ET type from the planet Klyptzyxm, he debuted in a 1944 *Superman* comic book.

SERMONS

● *The Yellow Brick Trail of Tears*

The last time I looked the sites referred to were still on the Internet. But I have noticed some very elaborate sites suddenly cease to be. Poof! Written on the ether. An ominous signal, perhaps, for any evidentiary trail.

Guy Grand (in *The Magic Christian*, Random House, 1960) spends a wad of money essentially paying people on the street to trash their own dignity, much like on the fun shows we see on TV today. But he also indulges in perhaps subtler and more private pranks. For example, in the film *Mrs. Miniver* he inserts a three-second close shot of a pen knife in the hand of Walter Pidgeon, its blade flashing a glint from the fireplace. Pidgeon has just opened and read a note from Greer Garson, and his eyes are apparently fixed on the glintful blade. In the mind of the audience, this almost subliminal shot implants a message of murderous intent that leads nowhere, and at the conclusion of the film the viewers are puzzled without realizing why. Of course Guy Grand got a kick out of it, and presumably so did Terry Southern and his readers. I know I did. From the vantage of Guy Grand, this is "second-level humor."

Julius and Ethel Rosenberg were executed in an era of antiBolshevik fervor (1953) as agents of Soviet espionage. Gen. Dwight Eisenhower ("Ike") was President at the time. Joseph Stalin, *né* Djugashvili, was running the USSR until his death in March of that year.

● *Dummy Bilking*

Herman Hollerith developed the punch card used in the 1890 US Census, which was so successful that he founded a data processing equipment company that proved he was a better inventor than businessman. Thomas J. Watson joined the company, turned it around, and acquired it on Hollerith's retirement, renaming it IBM (International Business Machines, often in big blue hues, hence "Big Blue"). TJ's motto, posted in IBM offices everywhere:

> THINK

In March 2002 the Supreme Court, on a diss-the-TJ-maxim roll, decided that illegal aliens are not protected by US labor law.

Zeno was one of those thinkalot Greeks who posited that speedy Achilles could never catch up with a moving turtle because by the time he got to where the turtle *was,* the turtle would have advanced to another point. And on and on.

Billy Sunday was his real name. An early 20th century evangelist, mesmerizing, effective, and maybe even sincere. He said, "Whiskey and beer are all right in their place, but their place is in hell." Carrie Nation was a wellintending, cardcarrying WCTU lady of the same era who called herself a "bulldog running along at the feet of Jesus" as she smashed saloon after saloon in the Midwest.

Pogo 'Possum was a comicbook philosopher (1945-1973), the creation of Walt Kelly.

The 18th Amendment to the US Constitution outlawed alcoholic beverages. The 21st repealed the 18th. *Prosit.*

The Land o' Goshen was supposedly the choicest real estate of Pharaoh's Egypt, the fiefdom of Jacob & Sons, until the Exodus.

Charlton Heston, movie Moses, also official spokesman for the National Rifle Association for years. An effective man for a highly effective organization.

Cited Biblical references, according to King James:

John 2:6-10 (wedding at Cana) And there were set there six waterpots of stone .. containing two or three firkins apiece. Jesus saith unto them, Fill the waterpots with water. And they filled them up to the brim. And he saith unto them, Draw out now, and bear unto the governor of the feast. .. When the ruler of the feast had tasted the water that it was made wine, .. (he) called the bridegroom, And saith unto him, Every man at the beginning doth set forth good wine; and when men have well drunk, then that which was worse: but thou hast kept the good wine until now.

Luke 1:15: For he shall be great in the sight of the Lord, and shall drink neither wine nor strong drink; and he shall be filled with the Holy Ghost.

Romans 14:21 It is good neither to eat flesh, nor to drink wine, nor anything whereby thy brother stumbleth, or is offended, or is made weak.

I Timothy 5:23 Drink no longer water, but use a little wine for thy stomach's sake and thine often infirmities.

● ***The Stalin-Giuliani Dictum and the Roark-Rockefeller Syndrome***

"Alphas and Epsilons" refer to social classes described by Huxley in *Brave New World* (*op. cit.*).

George Washington Carver (1864-1943) carved his own niche in the hall of Heroes of Postwar Southern Economic Resurgency by devising industrial applications for the peanut. This significantly boosted Dixie agribusiness by making it feasible to rotate cotton crops with soil-enriching legumes. Peanuts? Just talk to Jimmy Carter. This is essentially why the South did rise again.

Cited:

Russian Literature Since the Revolution, edited by Joshua Kunitz (Boni & Gaer, 1948)

The Fountainhead, Ayn Rand (1943). Movie made in 1949. Gary Cooper is a Howard Roark spitanimage. Book, thusly abetted by Gary Cooper, has sold over SIX MILLION copies (but it's been six million years) and has always been in print, thanks in part to a sect of ultralibertarian groupies.

Columbia Encyclopedia, 2nd Ed. (1950), Clark Ansley, ed.

GLOSSARY of Foreignisms

These terms appear in the preceding pages. While most of them may be familiar, or in any event in context require no elaboration, at the risk of appearing on the one hand fatuous, or on the other patronizing, I trust that some readers might appreciate an effort made to facilitate the uplooking of a phrase or two. Of course, the words mean ultimately what the characters who uttered them thought they meant, which in some cases (Charles Bugby comes to mind) is what they look like in English. I admit to a touch of Bugbyness in my own makeup, in that I do like the resonance of foreign words and phrases, and the color I think they add to the text. But no apologies here. *I paint what I paint, said Rivera,* penned E.B. White, quoth Reneau.

Key: *A = Arabic, Am = Aramaic, D = Dari, F = French, G = German, H = Hebrew, I = Italian, L = Latin, R = Russian, S = Spanish, Y= Yiddish.*
n = noun, v = verb, adj = adjective, adv = adverb.

Where transliteration was necessary, some license exercised. Where definitions are multiple, only the one pertinent to the text is used.

Al hum dullilah (A) By the grace of God
Allah akbar (A) God is great
Allez-vous (F) (how are) you doing (lit: going)
Aquí me siento yo, con triste corazon, echo puro pedo, en lugar de cagazón
   (S) Here I sit all broken hearted, came to shit and only farted
Ars gratia artis (L) Art for art's sake
Au contraire (F) To the contrary
Audite (L) Listen

Beaucoup (F) Much
Bien (F) Well *adv*
Birria (S) Spicy mutton broth
Blanche Maison (Maison Blanche) (F) White House
Bleu (F) Blue
Bon (F) Good
Borrón y cuenta nueva (S) Erase and start over

Cabrón (S) Son-of-a-bitch
Caca (S) Poop *n*
Camarada (S) Comrade
Carpe (L) Seize
Chadari (D) Lady's loosefitting, onepiece fullbody suit

Champ (F) Field *n*
Chéri (F) Dear *n*
Cheveu (F) Hair
Cœur (F) Heart
Comment (F) How
Cuchillo (Cuch') (S) Knife

Dábale arroz a la zorra el abad (S) The abbot gave rice to the vixen
Deus vult (L) God wills (it)
Diem (L) Day
Discolpati (I) Explain yourself
Divertissement (F) diversion
Donde venden tacos es donde pones tu taquería, compadre
    (S) Where they are selling tacos is where you put your taco stand, old buddy

Enfant (F) Child
En province (F) In the boonies
Ensalada (S) salad
Esprit (F) Spirit

Famille (F) Family
Femmes (F) Women
Fenêtre (F) Window
Fille (F) Daughter
Finie (F) Finished
Frère (F) Brother

Goy (Y) Gentile
Grand-mère (F) Grandmother
Guerre (F) War

Haut (F) High
Hasta la vista (S) See you later

Image fantastique (F) Fantastic image
Inshaalha (A) So be it

J'Accuse (F) I Accuse
Je ne sais quoi (F) I don't know what

Kaif hallek (A) How are you

Kvetch (Y) Bitch *v*

Lagunilla (S) The swap meet place in Mexico City
La commedia e finita (I) That's all, folks
La maledizione (I) The curse
Liebfraumilch (G) a Rhine Valley wine

Maestro (S) Blackbelt (proficient fellow)
Mamacita (S) Babe
Mein (G) My
Mene (Am) Evaluated
Merci (F) Thanks
Merde (F) Shit
Mère (F) Mother
Miroir (F) Mirror
Moi (F) Me
Mon (F) My
Mort (F) Death
Mots (F) Words

Nada (S) Nothing
Naturellement (F) Naturally
Nez (F) Nose
No hay general quien resiste un cañonazo de billetes
  (S) There is no general who can stand up to a cannon blast of hard cash
Nous (F) Us
Nuance nouveau (F) New Twist
Nudnik (Y) Pest
Número (S) Number
Nyet (R) No

Oeil (F) Eye

Pantaletas (S) Panties
Percé (F) Pierced
Pierre (F) Stone
Plus joli (F) More attractive
Pulgas, con bombas atómicas no matarás (S) Don't kill fleas with atomic bombs
Pulque (S) Fermented cactus juice

Quomodo Litterae Religiosa Piis Scribere, a Sancto Ioanne
  (L) How To Write Religious Literature for the Devout, by St. John

Recherché (F) Sought after

Schmo (Y) Dolt
Schlep (Y) Drag *v*
Schmuck (Y) Prick *n*
Selah (H) exclamation of uncertain meaning dear to King David
Sentaderas (S) Fanny
Shikse (Y) Gentile chick
Siete (S) Seven
Sic Transit Gloria (L) Thus fades away the glory
Sombrero (S) Hat
Sortilège (F) Sorcery

Tekel (Am) Weighed
Tête (F) Head
Tía Pelucas (S) Auntie Hairpiece (snappy dresser from a Mexican soap opera)
Tout (F) All
Tout suite (F) At once
Tovarishch (R) Comrade
Traditore (I) Traitor
Tutto nel mondo è burla (I) All the world's a joke

Uno (S) One

Véritable (F) True
Victoire (F) Victory
Videte (L) Watch *v*
Vie (F) Life
Vineus tarzanus ex machina (L) Tarzan vine, appearing miraculously
Visita (S) Visit
Voilà (F) There!
Vous (F) You

Yeux (F) Eyes

Acknowledgments

I am indebted to my artful and perceptive son, Reneau Reneau-Santiago, for his fearless candor in parsing the inconsistencies in this volume (advice which was welcomed and usually acted upon), and for finding the time to prepare the artwork that so ably interprets what was in my head. The cover and *Songs* artwork is that of Eduardo del Río, "Rius," creator of *Los Supermachos*, *Los Agachados*, and author of an endless stream of popular books. This valiant *don* is not only an icon of contemporary Mexican culture, but more importantly, a limpid and outspoken conscience for all of us, and I am honored and you are most fortunate that he was able to prepare his sketches for this book.

I thank Ray Bradbury for his words of encouragement. You may notice a tip o' me topper to his *Marionettes, Inc.* in the *talentgang* conversation.

For sustained encouragement and support, I am grateful to my wife, Virgita, my daughters Roxanne and Hélène, son Rubén, and kids-in-law, Patricia and José.

For his roaring introduction, much indebted to "Simon Elron" am I, although this modest lion of literature has opted to enlair himself in pseudonym. What can I say? He took the time to read, criticize, and finally write a glowing preamble for my unhumble effort. Some day I hope to open his closet door and thank him in print.

Portions of material in these pages appeared originally in *The Torquasian Times, Mizzappe,* and *The Oxford Accent* (*1950-1953*). Most of the verse in *Songs* appeared in *Misanthropoesy* (1970). All unnew material has been upgraded, restuffed, and buffed for this new millenium edition.

Picture Credits

Most of the artwork appearing here was commissioned by the publisher for the contents of this anthology; this includes the pictures by Rius, Reneau Reneau-Santiago, and Dalí Nemecio. Some drawings and photographs for the introductions to *Conversations* and *Sermons* were taken from other sources, as were the backgrounds (with assistance from Adobe's *Photoshop Elements 2*) for the comic sketches by Reneau-Santiago in these two sections of this book. The publisher is grateful for the opportunity to reproduce these images in this volume. A complete listing of these other sources follows:

p. 13 from Bradley Smith's *Mexico, a History in Art* (Doubleday/Windfall, 1968). *Museo Nacional de Antropología e Historia de México.* Jaguar funerary urn, Oaxaca.

p. 24 background from Andràs Batta and Sigrid Neef's *Opera --- Composers, Works, Performers* (Könemaun Velogsgesellschaft, 1999). Reproduction rights: *Theaterwissenschaftliche Sammlung der Universität zu Köln (TWS).* Set design for *La Bohème* by Hein Heckroth from the Wolf Völker production, 1930.

p. 25 background from Batta, TWS, *op. cit.* Set design for *The Makropulos Case* by Ruodi Barth from the Walter Pohl production, 1961.

p. 63 from Harold Schonberg's *The Great Conductors* (Simon & Schuster, 1967). In the New York Public Library collection. *Berlioz and His Orchestra.*

pp. 61-65 background from Batta, TWS, *op. cit.* Set design for *Simon Boccanegra* by Eduard Löffler from the 1941 *Teatro Municipal* production in Rio de Janeiro.

pp. 78-79 background from Jules Verne's *Hector Servadac* (Scribner, Armstrong, 1878). Engravings by C. Laplante.

pp. 116-117 background from Batta, TWS, *op. cit.* Set design for *Erwartung* by Alfred Siercke from the Günther Rennert production, 1954.

p. 155 Princess Ozma, from L. Frank Baum's *Emerald City of Oz* (Reilly & Lee, 1910). Drawing by John R. Neill.
Chief Joseph, from an original oil painting by Reneau Reneau-Santiago, 1978.

p. 156 background from L. Frank Baum's *John Dough and the Cherub* (Reilly & Britton, 1906). Drawing by Jno. R. Neill.

p. 165 Carrie Nation, photograph from record album cover, Douglas Moore's *Carrie Nation* (Desto Records, 1968).

p. 166 background from *John Dough, op. cit.*

p. 186 background from *John Dough, op. cit.*

Misanthropology is dedicated to my talented granddaughter, Dalí Xitlali Nemecio, whose enthusiasm and cheerfulness were a constant challenge to the thesis of this book. Or do I detect a glint of pessimism in that *roze in a pot of cold soyl?*

we blow in the
wind shwish
shwish shwish
we smell like a
roze in a pot
of cold soyl.

by Dali

Biographical Note

In his hour upon the stage, Reneau H Reneau developed a repertory that included appearances strutting as preacher's son and then PFC; sawing the air as U.S. History teacher and computer instructor; fretting as programmer and systems analyst, and bellowing as judgmental welfare case worker. Venues include Ft. Lewis, Maryland, Mexico, and California. In the fifties he edited and contributed to *The Torquasian Times* in Santa Cruz, and *The Oxford Accent*, in Berkeley. While in Mexico City in the seventies, he wrote and published *Programación de Computadoras*, and *Misanthropoesy*. He is retired and lives in Southern California.

Days of *Ensalada*
Mexico City, 1956

Bonus page for jaded commuters

Following Algebra I problem was said to be a favorite of Tolstoi:
A certain kulak had two tracts of land for his wheatfields, one being
half the size of the other. One day he sent his serfs to reap the wheat,
all of them going to the larger tract. At midday, he sent half to work
on the smaller field, the remainder continuing where they were. At
the end of the day, those at the bigfield sickled down the last spike
just as the whistle blew, but a patch still remained over at the halfplot.
The next day, a single serf was sent to finish the job, which he did;
again, just as the gohome whistle blew. Assume, of course, that
"midday" is exactly half the workday, and discount any traveltime
from bigfield to littlefield. The ergability (i.e. output) of these serfs is
exactly the same for eachandevery one. How many serfs were there?

The Gleanin' Ladies by J-F Millet

Congratulations for making it to this page! It is, of course, particularly gratifying for me, an unhumble misanthrope, to find you here, presumably having digested my grumpy collage, still turning pages, hungry for more grump. Statistics suggest that the most illumined of those who survive this marathon will write to the Nobel Committee recommending the author for a gold medal. Do you know what I say to that? Bah, humbug, I say. As I am sure you will concur, these pages are not dedicated to shilling this notion or that; no Willkie buttons, no Perot bumper stickers in view. The book just grumbles along, doesn't it? -- smashing through sacred calf and golden cow, scaling contrivance and artifice, arriving at some pretty amazing dead ends, eh? What th'! a cleverly conjured *deus ex machina*! Wowie! The bottom line is just to amuse and hackleraise, always with a sneer.

My course is ended, comrade. But you don't get off so easily. As is the case with any undergraduate course, there is a final exam, which appears opposite. Turn in the answers with your next U.S. History assignment. Extra credit for piglatin.